An Archdemon's Dilemma: How to Love Your Elf Bride Volume 4

Fuminori Teshima

Illustrations by COMTA

An Archdemon's Dilemma: How to Love Your Elf Bride Volume 4
by Fuminori Teshima

Translated by Hikoki
Edited by DxS

First published in Japan in 2018
Publication rights for this English edition arranged through Hobby Japan, Tokyo.

Find more books like this one at www.j-novel.club!

President and Publisher: Samuel Pinansky
Managing Editor: Aimee Zink

ISBN: 978-1-7183-5703-7
Printed in Korea
First Printing: March 2020
10 9 8 7 6 5 4 3 2 1

Contents

"Mashter Zagan, please look, a whole lot of acorns fell down over here!"

The young girl who came running over with a pitter-patter had acorns of various sizes clenched in both her fists. And in response, Zagan looked back at her with a muddled expression on his face. He could not decide whether to praise her or be anxious. However, Zagan was not a man with a good countenance by any standard. In fact, he had such a grim neutral expression that even adults trembled in fear, yet this young girl simply smiled back at him.

After thinking for a bit, Zagan nodded with an 'Mm' and picked up one of the acorns from the young girl's hands.

"This large one is an acorn from a sawtooth oak. It's extremely bitter, so it's better not to put it in your mouth unless you're starving."

"You can eat acorns?" The young girl stared back at him blankly and tilted her head to the side as she questioned him.

"Yeah. Though, I doubt there's anyone out there who would enjoy the taste. Plus, if you aren't careful when cooking them, even the better ones will put you through something terrible."

In truth, back in his days as a waif, Zagan went to the forest and tried cooking up whatever acorns he managed to gather. And, the moment he thought his stomach was full, he was assaulted by a terrible stomachache that had him in death throes.

When he reminisced about his past, enduring the desire to sigh over such bitter memories all the while, the young girl's eyes sparkled even brighter.

"Mashter Zagan, that's amazing! You know everything, don't you?"

"I don't know everything, I just know what I know."

His memory of getting lost in a forest and chewing on acorns was by no means a happy one. And yet, hearing about it made the young girl stare at the acorns fixedly.

"...What does it taste like, I wonder?"

"I'll just tell you right now, they taste horrible..." Zagan let out a sigh and picked one up as he said that. He could tell the girl was liable to chew on an acorn if he didn't step in. And so, even though he seemed to be bluntly refusing her, Zagan walked to the kitchen, put on an apron, and pulled out a frying pan. Before Nephy arrived at his castle, Zagan ate nothing but dry meat and milk, but that wasn't because he couldn't cook. On the contrary, having some sort of culinary skill was a life or death matter when one had to live off what little scraps of food they could find.

"Mashter Zagan, I love you so much!" The young girl exclaimed as she embraced Zagan.

"M-Mmm..." Zagan had to expend all his effort just to return a bewildered nod. And as he stood there awkwardly, a young girl with dragon horns tottered up to his side. It was Zagan's adopted daughter, Foll.

"Let me help, Zagan."

"Sorry about that. I'll leave it to you..." Zagan was honestly thankful that there was someone there to do a taste test. After all, knowing how to cook and knowing how to prepare a delicious meal were two completely different things.

9

"Can you also cook?" The young girl inquired, clearly impressed as she watched Foll get to work in the kitchen.

"A bit…" Nephy was in charge of preparing all meals, but Foll had been assisting her since she moved in. Recently, she had even taken charge of several items on the menu.

"Big Shish, you're also amazing!" The young girl hopped in place and raised her voice, obviously impressed by the revelation.

"Big Sis…!" Foll staggered upon being called 'Big Sis.' And, in an unusual turn, her cheeks flushed red as she stared at the girl in wonder. That made total sense. After all, Foll was doted on by those around her, but she had never done the same for anyone else. Sure, she was a dragon who had been alive for much longer than most humans, but she still looked and acted like a little girl.

"So cute…" Foll said as she hugged the young girl tight.

"Huh?" The young girl's eyes darted about for a bit, but she immediately put on a smile with an 'eheheh' as she returned Foll's embrace.

"Big Shish, you're warm."

"Zagan, I feel like… it's fine to leave things like this," Foll claimed as she rubbed her cheek into the girl and let out a satisfied sigh.

"Mmm… Agreed."

"No, that's no good! Both of you, come to your senses at once!"

An astonished voice resounded in the room while the two of them had their eyes partially closed in satisfaction. It was none other than Chastille, fully equipped with her Anointed Armor for the first time in a while.

"Nephy's turned into a child! There's no way it's fine to leave things like this!" Chastille yelled, seemingly on the verge of tears as her red hair swayed in the wind.

The young girl embracing Foll with an innocent smile was clearly no more than five years old. However, she had pointy ears, snow-white hair, and azure eyes. It was clear as day that she was a high elf. And, most curiously, she had an oversized collar around her neck.

Yes, the child was very obviously the same woman Zagan couldn't help but love… Nephy.

Nephy had turned into a child, the Archdemon was wearing an apron while cooking up acorns, and Chastille was keeping things together. Anything and everything about the situation was absolutely impossible.

Zagan's group was currently within a destroyed elven village. More precisely, it was Nephy's hometown in Norden.

As for the cause of the strange situation they found themselves in… Well, two days ago—

Chapter I ✡ Our Family Has Grown, so It's Time to Visit My Bride's Home!

"Nephy's... not here?" Zagan was walking about his own castle, looking for the love of his life. Though it was once a castle with torture devices and skeletons scattered all over the place, thanks to Nephy's hard work, it had become so beautiful that it was beyond recognition. Since the torn ceilings and such were repaired, nowadays it was an environment that could house several dozen people. Plus, many sorcerers traveled through the castle often.

About a month had gone by since the evening ball that Archdemon Bifrons held. During that incident, dozens of the sorcerers in attendance had lost their lives. The one who managed to get the situation under control was Zagan, and because of that, no fewer than thirty sorcerers ended up pledging their allegiance to him.

Thanks to that incident, he learned that the girl he loved, Nephy, was of a race called 'high elves.' All members of that race understood Celestian and could perform celestial mysticism to some degree. However, he did not know much else. Getting to the bottom of the mystery would take far more manpower than Zagan had.

As he took a peek into a room, Zagan spotted an old woman with goat horns stirring some kind of syrupy liquid inside an iron pot.

"Keeheehee, keeheeheeheeheeheehee, just you wait, Valefor. There are none who sip upon my chocolate fondant who continue to resist me. Keeheeheeheehee."

Is she making sweets for Foll...? This suspicious old woman was Gremory. She possessed the second name Enchantress and was powerful enough to be considered an Archdemon candidate. Due to that, she was either ranked first or second among Zagan's subordinates... Though, she looked more like a granny engrossed in making treats for her granddaughter at present.

Celestian, celestial mysticism, Sacred Swords, the Sigils of the Archdemon, and the thirteen Archdemons. There were far too many obstacles that Zagan had to overcome.

The new sorcerers under his rule were supporting Zagan's research, and coming and going between the preceding Archdemon Marchosias' Archdemon Palace and Zagan's castle to search for the information he desired.

Sorcerers barely understood the idea of cooperation, but the reason they never quarreled under Zagan was in large part because of one particular individual.

"Put in some work, you lot! Find the books my liege is searching for!"

A butler with the terrifying face of a man-eating fiend was raising his voice in the entrance hall. The elderly man's left arm was artificial and made of armor, and he had a sword stowed away at his waist. He was the natural enemy of sorcerers, a wielder of a Sacred Sword... ex-Archangel Raphael. Since he was serving Zagan's household as a butler, he was spurring the sorcerers to work.

"Today's lunch is pork bone soup with lamb. If you want to settle in and eat it, then carry out your damned duties through to the end!" Raphael exclaimed, his hand gripping a ladle from the kitchen instead of his Sacred Sword. It seemed he had finished his preparations for lunch and was trying to use that fact to motivate the sorcerers.

13

"OOOH!" In response, the sorcerers raised their voices without even a hint of agitation.

His outer appearance and past actions were unbearable, but Raphael's cooking was superb. It was more than good enough to capture the hearts of people who had been eating it for over a month. Plus, since he spent a large portion of his life as an Archangel, he possessed enough combat prowess to exterminate all the sorcerers gathered here in a head-on battle. As such, Zagan tried to see what would happen if he left assembling the sorcerers to that elderly butler, and luckily, it turned out quite well. Though, there may have been one other reason that things worked out so well...

Unexpectedly, even sorcerers won't bite the hand that feeds them... Zagan had arranged for each of them to be given something they desired in exchange for their assistance. He paid them in gold, grimoires, catalysts used for sorcery, and the like. As long as they didn't betray him, he continued to pay them at fixed intervals. Thanks to that, even though thirty renowned sorcerers were gathered in one place, not a single quarrel had broken out.

"Well if it isn't my liege. Do you need something of me?" Raphael made a sweeping motion as he bent at the waist, taking notice of Zagan's entrance.

"No, I'm looking for Nephy. Is she in the kitchen?"

"If you're looking for Lady Nephy, I believe she went off to the archives after she got back from her shopping trip."

"No, I just came from there and didn't bump into her. Did we miss each other?" Zagan tilted his head to the side in confusion at the situation.

"It's almost time for lunch, so I doubt she would have left the castle," Raphael replied.

15

"Got it. I'll try searching a little more," Zagan said, leaving Raphael behind as he continued his quest to locate Nephy.

Since it was close to noon, he came across sorcerers sporadically dashing down the hallways. Having said that, sorcerers were natural loners, so even when he passed them in the corridor, their exchanges only ever amounted to a slight nod, which left the inside of his castle just as quiet as before.

"Ah, Mister Zagan, gooooood mooooooorning!"

The one who let out such a noisy and headache-inducing voice wasn't a sorcerer.

"...Wait. Why the hell are you here?" Zagan asked as he firmly grasped the head of the girl who was passing by him. It was the siren girl who he'd saved during Bifrons' evening ball. Unlike the rest of them, she was a singer from a musical troupe, not a sorcerer.

"I mean, like, weren't all the members of the band and their instruments totally gobbled up in that boat fight? Anyway, I was, like, unwinding at a bar, and Big Sis Manuela told me to go to your castle!"

That damn woman... Does she take my place for a daycare or something? Zagan was suddenly struck with a headache due to that thought. Even as a joke, doing something like sending her off to look for a job at an Archdemon's castle was out of the question... Maybe Manuela trusted Zagan, but if it were any of the other Archdemons, then the siren would've already been turned into a sacrifice or lab rat.

"I never heard anything about that... Honestly, I'm surprised you got in here..." Zagan had put several barriers in place around his castle. An average sorcerer or Angelic Knight wouldn't even have noticed the place, and if one were to actually spot it, they'd be assaulted by pain that stopped just short of killing them. Fact of the matter was, a regular person who wasn't even a sorcerer surviving to face him was impossible.

"All I did was, like, follow Miss Nephy while we were chatting…"

"Really… I'm surprised you managed that."

"Huh?"

It wasn't just the path up to his castle that was booby-trapped, but even the inside. If this girl triggered even one of them, she would have died instantly, but somehow she didn't.

"Y-You're kidding, right?" The siren questioned, face pale after learning the truth.

"Let me ask you a question instead. Do you really think an Archdemons' castle wouldn't have any traps in it?"

"That's, you know… Since it's someone like Mister Zagan who went and saved a lowly commoner like me, I thought, like, this would be a safe space or something…"

"This isn't a safe space, you careless nitwit. If such a kind Archdemon truly existed, then they would already be dead."

A sorcerer's base was a treasure trove of knowledge. And to sorcerers, knowledge equaled power, so leaving their base exposed was the same as asking to have their power stolen. That was why a burglar, of all things, was a sorcerer's greatest fear. Naturally, in order to protect themselves from would-be thieves, sorcerers setup countless terrifying traps.

Even Zagan, who was fairly indifferent in that regard, had set up severe traps that would activate when outsiders were present. More specifically, his traps were so deadly that Barbatos, an Archdemon candidate, would have had a hard time surviving. Although, protecting his knowledge mattered little to Zagan. No, what he truly wished to protect was his family… Nephy, Foll, and Raphael.

"N-No way! Aren't we, like, on super good terms, Mister Zagan!? Please save meeeeee!" The siren wailed as she clung to Zagan, her face pale.

"Like I care. I don't even know your name."

"It's Selphy! Please at least remember my naaame!"

Forget remembering it, he had never even heard it in the first place.

"For the time being, hold onto this," Zagan said as he handed over a bead-sized jewel to Selphy the siren, letting out a sigh.

"What's this?"

Honestly, Selphy was so annoying that he didn't really want to get involved with her, but if she was Manuela's acquaintance, he couldn't just leave her to die. That woman was Nephy's friend. Plus, they often relied on her to find suitable clothes for himself, Nephy, and Foll. Sure, the weird clothes she forced on them whenever they let their guard down was a bother, but it was also true that she was one of the few people who could talk to him normally.

Eventually, Selphy vigorously nodded her head up and down. And while he gazed at the siren with an exasperated look on his face, Zagan suddenly tilted his head to the side.

"Now that I think of it, what's with your feet? Are they artificial?"

A siren's lower body was akin to the tail of a snake. However, Selphy had two legs sprouting out like an ordinary human.

"Ah, these? This castle's awfully dry, so it kinda ends up like this."

"…You lot grow legs when it's too dry?"

"Sure do, what about it?"

Zagan's head began to ache again as he heard her oblivious reply.

"So wait, since Manuela told you to come here… do you plan on working for me?"

"Yup! I heard you were, like, totally short on hands."

"It's true that I'm short on hands, but… do you have any knowledge of sorcery?"

"Nope! I mean, I've got, like, nothing but songs in my head!" Selphy claimed in a boastful tone… Well, that made sense since she was a singer, but it didn't seem useful to Zagan at all.

Still, left with no choice, Zagan pointed to the direction he came from.

"There's a butler named Raphael in the entrance hall. Go and see if he has a job for you. If he doesn't, just give up and go home."

Keeping this girl around seemed like more trouble than it was worth, but he felt awkward turning away one of Bifrons' victims. And so, he decided to at least give her a single chance.

"Yaaay! Thanks, Mister Archdemon!" Selphy jumped for joy at his approval, and as he watched her, Zagan suddenly recalled something important.

"Wait, you said you were walking with Nephy, right? Do you know where she went?"

"Oh, seemed like she was heading to the garden."

"I see. You have my thanks," Zagan said. Then, he turned his back on Selphy and began walking toward the garden.

"Whoa… Mister Archdemon just gave me his 'thanks'…"

He never noticed Selphy letting out a bewildered voice.

When he reached the garden, Zagan found a single beast curled up, basking in the sun. It let out a loud yawn as if it were comfortable, but for a cat, it was a little… no, it was bizarrely large. It was, in fact, a lion with a large build and black fur.

When I look at him like this... he really does seem like a cat, huh...? Zagan, of all people, felt the urge to pet his fur every now and then, but he resisted. After all, he was not looking at a lion. No, he faced an Archdemon candidate, a sorcerer who held the second name Black Blade, Kimaris.

"Kimry, Kimry..." A young girl called out as she tottered on over toward him. She seemed just shy of ten years old. Her green hair was tied up in braids that ran along her back, she had large amber eyes, and she was wearing the native dress of some foreign country that used white and scarlet as the main colors. However, strangest of all were the dragon horns poking out of the gaps in her hair.

Yes, she was Zagan's adopted daughter, Foll. Her true identity was Apparition Valefor, a former Archdemon candidate.

"Haaah... Excuse me, what's the matter, little lady?" Kimaris asked as he turned his golden eyes over to Foll.

"The flowers in the flowerbed are blooming. Come look."

"I see. Very well, let's go," Kimaris replied smoothly using human speech. Then, the black lion began to walk briskly on his four legs, and Foll rode on top of him as if it were perfectly natural.

Zagan hesitated, wondering whether he should interrupt them, but he was searching for Nephy, so he quietly trailed them. Before long, the lion came to a stop near a growth of beautiful pink flowers.

"They sure have bloomed beautifully, haven't they, little lady?"

"It's 'cause I gave them snake blood every day."

"How admirable. Well then, shall we harvest them?"

"Mmm... Yeah," Foll nodded in agreement as she accepted Kimaris' request. In response, the black lion began growling in a deep voice. From the outside, it looked like an innocent girl was being menaced by a beast of prey, but Foll didn't show even a hint of fear. Instead, she gripped the stem of the freshly blooming flower

with all her might. And then, just as Zagan was wondering what she was doing, she vigorously yanked it out.

"AAAAAAAAAAAAAAAAAAAAAAAAAAAAAAAAAAAAH!"

Immediately following that, a shriek that made him want to cover his ears rang out. Upon taking a closer look, Zagan noticed that the root of the flower Foll yanked out had a human-like shape, and the shriek had come out of its mouth.

"Look Kimry, it's huge!" Foll claimed as she let out a sigh of satisfaction.

"You sure raised it well. For a moment, I panicked and thought I wouldn't be able to neutralize it in time."

The human-shaped root was large enough to be an armful for Foll. In fact, it was about the size of a human baby. This plant was called a mandrake. It was something that was often used as an ingredient in potions, and the moment it was pulled from the earth, it shrieked out a curse. Any regular person who heard that shriek would die, and it was even atrocious enough to drive most sorcerers mad.

Kimaris seemed to specialize in sorcery related to sound, so it appeared he was taking care of blocking off the mandrake's shriek.

"You're worrying too much, Kimry. No way a mandrake's scream can break through a dragon's mana!" Foll proclaimed as she shook her head in derision.

Foll may have been young, but she was still a dragon. Dragons possessed natural resistance to all curses and sorcery, so they were able to easily repel the shriek of a mandrake.

"It is not like all the sorcerers here have the same power as you or I, little lady. They are also Sir Zagan's subordinates, so we must ensure their safety."

"Mmm... That's why I brought you along, Kimry."

"That was very admirable of you, little lady."

After that, the two of them turned to Zagan.

"Did you need something, Sir Zagan?"

"Yeah, I'm just looking for Nephy…"

"Well, I saw her heading toward the throne room. It looked like she was searching for you, Sir Zagan."

"Really…? Thanks for the tip. I'll go take a look, then."

It seemed that she was also searching for him, and they missed each other yet again. After he thanked Kimaris, Zagan looked over to his daughter. The adorable young girl was cradling the large mandrake as if it were precious.

"Foll, what are you using that for?"

"A snack," Foll replied without hesitation, which left Zagan at a sudden loss for words.

"…I see. Is it tasty?"

"Mmm… It's packed full of sweet mana and tastes really good!"

Now that she mentioned it, Zagan recalled that there was apparently an incident where a mandrake field a sorcerer was raising was devoured by a dragon. It wasn't very well known, but perhaps they were a dragon's favorite food.

"Well, that's good… Could it be… that your usual meals aren't enough for you?"

Foll appeared to be just a small girl, but her original form was more than large enough to fit a human rider as she soared through the sky. Despite that, she still had a petite build for a dragon, so he assumed they had been feeding her enough. However, his human standards for meals may have misled him.

"Nuh-uh. Nephy's food is delicious, and I get more than enough of it. It's just, I'm weak, so I have to build up my mana."

She called herself weak, but Foll was strong enough to easily beat any run-of-the-mill sorcerer. That probably meant she wanted to grow as a dragon.

"Zagan, do you want some, too?" Foll asked as she stuck her large mandrake out toward him.

"…Maybe later," Zagan responded. And after patting her head one last time, he spun on his heels and walked over to the throne room.

Upon returning to the throne room, Zagan found Raphael and Selphy there… and he had no idea what she was guilty of, but Selphy was pale and trembled as Raphael grasped the scruff of her neck.

"My liege, we have an intruder. Shall I dispose of her, or would you prefer I hand her over to those damn subordinates of yours?"

Raphael was a man who had cut down close to five hundred sorcerers in self-defense, so he created misunderstandings and prejudice as he walked about. Selphy, on the other hand, was the type of person who clearly didn't listen to what others were saying. Logically, there was no way the two of them would share any sort of proper conversation.

I should have predicted it would end up like this… He normally would have noticed, but he hadn't really been paying attention to others since he was out looking for Nephy.

"Ah… It seems Nephy picked her up. Do you have some kind of job you can give her?"

"Hmm, so you plan to put her to work here?"

"Is that not possible?"

"It's not impossible, but I cannot guarantee this fellow will survive."

"Eeeeeek," Selphy shrieked and trembled, but Zagan nodded like it didn't really matter.

"If we inform my subordinates that Selphy isn't fodder or a toy, no one will touch her."

"Then there is no problem. I shall impress what it means to work for Archdemon Zagan into her very soul."

"Actually, I'll just head home! I'm fine being unemployed, really!"

"You fool. You have already come into the service of my liege. Put your damn life on the line and work."

"NOOOOOOOOOOOOOOOO!"

He's actually saying that he'll teach her everything she needs to know to do her job, right...? Though he sensed the true meaning of Raphael's words, Zagan remained silent and took a seat atop his throne. It would have been fine for him to dispel the misunderstanding, but if she truly planned on working at his castle, it was better for her to get used to it. That was why he decided to leave it be. And just as that uproar worsened...

"Master Zagan, are you in the middle of something?"

A voice as melodious as a chime called out to him. And when he turned his gaze toward the source, he saw Nephy standing at the entrance to the throne room. She was wearing her usual ultramarine one piece dress and apron combo, the outfit of a maid, and there was a boorish collar around her neck. Her snow-white hair went down to her waist, and her eyes were azure like a serene lake.

Nephy's pointy ears were a racial trait of elves, but while this girl was an elf, she was also far more. She was actually the descendant of an ancient species called high elves. And on top of that, she was the woman Zagan couldn't help but love.

24

Oh, right, Nephy was also searching for me... Nephy may have had something important to discuss. And so, Zagan shook his head and replied to her.

"No, I've concluded my business. Don't worry about it."

"I see..." Nephy tilted her head to the side, clearly puzzled at the sight of Selphy's face, which was a mess of tears and mucus.

"Mizz Nephy, zaaaaaaaaaaaafe meeeeeeeeeeee."

"Ah, I ended up hiring her to help Raphael out."

For a moment after Nephy heard Zagan's explanation, she remained expressionless and the tips of her ears happily quivered. Then, she clapped her hands together.

"Good for you, Miss Selphy."

"Are you, like, even listening to me at all?" Selphy's expression sank into despair as she questioned whether she had any allies left in this place.

"Preparations for lunch are complete, but will you be having it later?" Raphael asked Zagan, ignoring Selphy completely.

"Yeah. You can eat without us."

Naturally, he had been searching for Nephy because he had business with her. And since he wished to discuss a fairly delicate matter that could take long, he didn't want to make the other sorcerers wait.

"As you wish," Raphael said as he put his hand to his chest and bowed.

"It seems like you've been searching for me," Zagan claimed as he beckoned Nephy over. Zagan also had something he wished to talk about, but he wanted to hear what she had to say first.

"Yes. There's something... that I would like to speak with you about."

"...I see. For the time being, take a seat."

25

"Understood…" Nephy said as she walked up to the front of Zagan's throne. And then, just like that, she plunked her butt down onto Zagan's lap.

Ignoring Selphy, who appeared stunned by her action, Nephy tilted her head to the side.

"Like this?"

"Mmm, very well."

"That's oka— Oomph!?"

Zagan thought Selphy was making some sort of commotion, but by the time he looked over to her, Raphael had already sealed her mouth.

There were other chairs in the corners of the throne room, but Nephy showed no hesitation as she plunked down on Zagan's lap. And yet, she was still leaning forward to put more weight on her feet and not overburden Zagan, which he found so charming. However, Zagan also felt his face start to contort due to the feeling of her soft butt and thighs.

I feel like Nephy has been behaving a lot more spoiled lately…

Ever since the incident with Bifrons, Nephy had lost all reservations about sitting on Zagan's lap. It seemed like she no longer even held any doubts about it.

After basking in the situation for a moment, Zagan directed a hearty nod at Raphael, who took Selphy and left the throne room.

"Holy crap. Mister Archdemon is a pretty generous guy."

"The extent of my liege's thoughtfulness is not something that we can surmise."

"So what, you're not sure how deep it goes?" Selphy was clamoring about something right until the end, but it probably wasn't something Zagan had to concern himself with.

After the two of them walked off into the distance, Zagan looked over to Nephy. She was fiddling with her hair using her fingers, seemingly conflicted about something. Her pointy ears were gradually drooping, and after jumping back up stiffly for an instant, they would simply droop again. It was rather apparent that she had worked up the courage to talk to him, but it seemed like her nerves got the better of her each time she tried to speak her mind.

Hmm, maybe I should try to calm her down somehow?

He wasn't in a hurry. No, he simply wished to encourage the girl he loved. And so, after worrying about it for a while, Zagan scooped up some of Nephy's hair. Then, he tried to brush it against the strands Nephy was fiddling with.

"Huh…?"

"…"

Nephy's ears quivered in surprise, and she looked up at Zagan. Apparently, she had not expected such an action from him. And honestly, even Zagan couldn't explain why he did such a thing, so the two of them just ended up staring at each other silently.

Now that I take a good look at it, her hair is actually transparent, isn't it? Mmm… How beautiful. The pigment had faded, and it was basically transparent. Seemed it only looked white because it was all bunched together.

Nephy hung her head down as if deliberating something, and then nodded as if she had thought up a brilliant idea. Following that, she leaned back into Zagan's chest and used the tips of the hair she was fiddling with to brush Zagan's neck.

Huh? What's with this situation? I mean, I can't complain, but…

In any case, Nephy was extremely cute as she tried to tickle Zagan with a serious expression on her face. He just wanted to hug her tightly right away. However, the Archdemon simply reclined

27

back into his throne, playing with his bride's hair all the while, as Nephy continued tickling his neck.

A rather awkward silence stretched out for quite a while as the two figures continued their actions. And the first one to break that silence… was Zagan.

"That tickles…"

"…Should I stop?"

"No, it's fine, keep going."

Even Zagan himself didn't know what was 'fine' about it, but it didn't feel bad. Or rather, it felt warm and comfortable to him. And after that continued for a while longer, Nephy finally worked up her courage and opened her mouth to speak.

"Master Zagan, in truth, I have come to make an earnest request of you."

It was the first time Nephy had done anything like this, and she was being so formal to boot. Confused by her, Zagan tensed up as he nodded back to her.

"Hm… Let's hear it."

Nephy took a deep breath when she heard his response. The feeling of her chest swelling up with her sweet breath was directly passed on to him, which made Zagan reflexively wrap his arms around her back.

Nephy's body trembled with a twitch, but she still opened her mouth, fighting back her nerves.

"Could you… allow me to take a leave of absence for a short while?" Nephy was making a request to leave Zagan's side, which should have made Zagan sink into depression. However, he instead cut right to the chase without being agitated at all.

"I see… So you want to go and investigate the elven village, then?"

"...H-Huh?" Nephy's mouth flapped open and closed. She was shocked, as Zagan seemed to have read her mind.

"H-How did you figure that out?"

"I can tell just by looking, right?"

"Is that so..." Nephy still seemed to be quite bewildered, but her ears were standing up as if she was somehow relieved.

I mean, I was looking for her because I wanted to invite her to travel there together... It had already been a month, but because of a chance meeting with Archdemon Bifrons, Nephy found out that she was a high elf. In addition, she found out that the Celestian language only she was able to understand were the words of the high elves. That revelation sure made her want to rush out of the castle right away, but due to all the new subordinates Zagan had gained, she instead waited until the housework around the castle could be managed by the staff.

Once in a while, her ears made it clear that she was troubled... Zagan wanted to fulfill her desires as soon as possible, but he was not used to relying on strangers. It took quite some time until he was convinced that he had nothing to worry about with his new subordinates. And that newfound knowledge was why Zagan replied nonchalantly.

"I've been thinking now's the right time to take you there, Nephy."

"By take me there... you mean you will be coming as well, Master Zagan?"

"There are guys like Bifrons running about, so I can't just let you go on your own," Zagan said, then turned to look over to the door Raphael left through and continued, "Fortunately, those new subordinates of mine are obedient. Leaving the castle in Raphael's capable hands should be enough."

If Zagan were to leave for the hidden village, then the castle would be missing its master, so only Raphael could take charge.

"Master Zagan, you've seen through everything, haven't you?"

"Not everything."

"I will accompany you… no matter where you go. No matter where it is… please take me along, Master Zagan."

"I-I shall…" Zagan said, returning an exaggerated nod to her. At that exact moment, a sudden thought popped into his mind.

Nephy's birthplace… huh?

It may have been a place full of painful memories to Nephy, but he was overjoyed by the idea of visiting the place where she grew up.

And just like that, Zagan's household ended up following Nephy on her visit home.

"Hmph… So this is the castle Nephy is staying in?"

A lone girl was floating in the sky above Zagan's castle. Her hair was silver bordering on white, and she had eyes that shone like the moon. She was a dark elf with swarthy skin who wore a rather risque outfit. Also, her face was astonishingly similar to Nephy's. The girl's name was Nephteros. She was Archdemon Bifrons' servant, a high elf who hated Nephy.

Nephelia… That girl who had the same face as her. Even though they were both supposedly high elves, Bifrons valued Nephelia more. And that fact made embers of hatred burn within Nephteros' heart.

If she were to launch a surprise attack from here and throw in her sorcery, even an Archdemon would be unable to protect Nephelia. And in that moment, Nephteros had the ideal opportunity to launch her assault. Or that was the case, but…

"What a lucky woman…" Nephteros had not come to kill Nephelia. If she launched an attack against the castle, she would no longer be able to accomplish her true goal. That was why all she could do was glare at the castle in an annoyed manner.

Nephteros had something wrapped around her arm. *As soon as I finish delivering this, I won't have any more business with this annoying castle…*

The castle below her eyes had a countless number of powerful barriers delicately arranged around it. The fundamentals of sorcery involved drawing magic circles. By reading and understanding grimoires, those magic circles could be enhanced.

Remarkably, the barrier surrounding Zagan's castle made use of the surrounding forest and wove it in as a portion of the barrier. The position of much of the trees and brooks was easy enough to utilize, but the shadows cast by the moon and the sun, and even the sound of the wind blowing through the forest, were all functioning as part of the magic circle. In other words, it was constructed so that the structure of the barrier changed depending on the time and the direction of the wind.

Any method of breaking through wouldn't work a second time. It was a fearsome barrier that had no real weakness.

I hate to admit it, but this sorcery is even artistic… Nephteros, who studied sorcery under Archdemon Bifrons, was unable to mimic it. It truly was the crystallization of Zagan's power. She was unintentionally fascinated by it.

A large number of sorcerers were bustling about in a hurry within that beautiful barrier. They were likely Zagan's subordinates, and each and every single one of them failed to notice their master's enemy in the skies right above them.

If she just threw down her 'package' like this, then she could take off, but…

"Urgh…" Nephteros felt a wave of bloodlust strike her body as she mulled over her thoughts. Looking down at the castle below her feet, she spotted an elderly man barking orders at the sorcerers. If she remembered correctly, he was a former Angelic Knight named Raphael.

Well, an Archdemon wouldn't employ only fools, I suppose.

Since he'd noticed her, she had no other choice. Nephteros unleashed her mana, which made the barrier oscillate slightly. Even if Zagan far surpassed her as a sorcerer, it was an enormous barrier that covered not only a castle, but an entire forest. Due to its massive size, the parts of it that could be compared to a person's joints were rather brittle. And so, there were definitely 'gaps' that most enemies would be unable to sense.

By making the barrier vibrate, Nephteros brought such a 'gap' to the surface. And just like that, she wove her way through it and descended toward the castle.

The sight of her figure as she unleashed a wave of mana and brazenly broke through an Archdemon's barrier was simply sublime. However, sweat crept up on her face instead of a satisfied smirk.

Faster! I have to get through before the barrier changes! Nephteros knew she would be caught in the barrier if the wind even shifted ever so slightly. After all, getting through his barrier was much like threading the eye of a needle, so even a gentle quiver would result in her failure.

She couldn't afford to be impatient. However, she had to struggle to get through even a second sooner. And as she battled against the powerful barrier, Nephteros finally realized what a terrifying enemy Archdemon Zagan was.

Before long, the other sorcerers began to raise their voices upon spotting her.

"Y-You're Bifrons'…!" "What are you planning now!?" "Calm down! This one's sorcery is powerful. If you carelessly pick a fight, she'll turn the tables on you."

Nephteros landed in front of Raphael, barely sparing the sorcerers who were making a ruckus a glance.

The one with the most power in this place… is this guy, huh? Nephteros didn't think he was stronger than her. However, he was someone that Zagan kept at his side. She couldn't afford to be lax.

Gazing at him, Nephteros formed a somewhat strained smile and shook back her silver hair in an overbearing manner. And then, she took on a resolute attitude and informed him of something rather shocking.

"Um, I came to return Zagan's mantle, but…"

At that, everyone present let out a sigh at once.

"That's freaking misleading. If you're gonna do that, then just come in through the door like normal!" "Now that I think of it, she was just that kinda girl, huh?" "Mmhmm. She can't just honestly give her thanks or anything, can she?" "Is it that? Is she finally admitting she wants to get along with little Nephy?" "Well, with how kind Nephy is, she'll definitely want to spend some time with this one."

Eventually, the sorcerers each returned to their work as if they had lost all interest in her. Nephteros shot a glance toward the sorcerers who were saying whatever they pleased, but even as she kept a composed expression, the tips of her ears were dyed red and quivering about.

After Raphael looked her over with a cold, calculated gaze, he abruptly turned his back on her.

"Follow me."

She wanted to return the mantle in a hurry and scurry back home, but her pride wouldn't allow her to turn her back here. And so, Nephteros reluctantly followed Raphael.

The place he led her to seemed to be a parlor. Raphael pulled out a chair and urged Nephteros to take a seat before going on to briskly prepare some beverages. Shortly after, he presented her with some tea that gave off a relieving scent.

"Have a drink."

"Ah, thanks…"

Nephteros unintentionally ended up bowing her head as she responded. Raphael's courteous actions had caught her off guard. After that, Raphael muttered something as he lined up some cookies to go with the tea.

"I'll tell you this before you say anything, but my liege is currently absent."

"Huh, he's not here?"

"Indeed."

Unable to hide her bewilderment, Nephteros questioned him again.

"Then… Um… What is this…?"

"I was commanded to give you the minimum amount of hospitality."

"Didn't he mean… to intercept and attack me?"

"You fool. My liege is a gentleman. He would never allow a guest to leave empty-handed."

Unable to understand what he was saying, Nephteros simply began blinking rapidly as her ears quivered lightly.

"But, just earlier, did you not direct your ire toward me when I was above the castle?"

"If someone suspicious was directly above you, would you not be on guard?"

"Suspicious, you say… Haven't we met before?"

"I am not a sorcerer. There's no way I can distinguish someone's face at such a distance," Raphael replied, shaking his head all the while.

"That's, um… Sorry. I didn't notice…"

"It is not something for you to pay any mind. More importantly, drink the damn tea before it gets cold."

"Thank you…" Nephteros' face remained bewildered as she raised her teacup.

For the time being… I'm their enemy, right…? It's not like Master Bifrons apologized to them or anything…

Nephteros' master was someone who would rather just up and die than bow their head to another. Bifrons was a being who would never apologize.

Though perhaps that was just normal for Archdemons, so Zagan understood. Was that why she was being treated with such kindness? Did he truly mean to entertain an enemy, not strike them down?

Nephteros tried a bite of one of the cookies in front of her as she mulled over such thoughts.

"This… is delicious…"

"…Has it caught your fancy?"

"I suppose it has… Did you make these?"

"Indeed."

Nephteros unintentionally let out a sigh. She thought that perhaps they were poisoned or something, but they were just normal, delicious cookies. Both the cookies and the tea were so delicious that Nephteros was left earnestly perplexed.

How did such a beastly man manage to make these...?

Raphael's face was terrifying enough to spur sorcerers to rush in and attack him out of fear. She couldn't possibly imagine him making sweets in the kitchen.

Nephteros didn't know a thing about baking sweets, but she had no confidence that she could make such delicious ones even if she did. On the other hand, she thought about making something terrible to harass Bifrons, but that Archdemon would surely see through her plans right away, so any effort would be in vain.

Nephteros made sure not to let any crumbs fall down on Zagan's mantle, which she had on her lap as she chewed on some cookies, and continued questioning Raphael.

"Where did Zagan go?"

"Lady Nephy's hometown. I've heard it takes a whole day to reach on the wings of a dragon. They'll be back in three days at the earliest, but I'm unsure when they plan to return."

"Is that so..." Nephteros stared down at Zagan's mantle.

What should I do? Even though I came all the way here, just leaving the mantle and taking off is kind of silly, isn't it...?

Having said that, it was too far away to just chase after him. In the worst case, they could even pass each other by. If that were to happen, she would be even more laughable. And while she was worrying about what to do, her teacup emptied.

Shaking her head at Raphael, who was offering to refill her tea, Nephteros stood up from her chair.

"I'll come again."

For the time being, I should at least give my thanks for last time in person.

During the incident on the boat, Zagan had saved Nephteros' life, but she had never properly thanked him. Also, thanks to the

'souvenir' that he gave her, she was even able to torment Bifrons. There was also the matter of his mantle, but she thought properly conveying her gratitude for such things was the most important part.

If I don't, then one day I'll end up like Master Bifrons…

Casual indifference may have been normal for sorcerers, but her feelings of wanting to reject becoming that kind of person were at the forefront of her mind.

"Wait. I have something to hand over to you. You may wait there for a moment," Raphael called out to Nephteros, stopping her in her tracks as she turned to leave.

"Huh…? Understood," Nephteros replied, then lounged about until Raphael's return.

"You may take these with you," Raphael said upon his return.

"What are they?"

Raphael held out a package. It was small enough to snugly fit into Nephteros' hand and was tied up with an adorable ribbon.

"They're just leftovers. Don't pay it any mind and just take them."

"By leftovers… do you mean more of the cookies I just ate?"

Raphael responded with an exaggerated nod. It seemed he had heard Nephteros muttering about how they were delicious, so he prepared them for her as a souvenir.

His kindness tugged at Nephteros' heartstrings. It felt like she was being toyed around with right until the very end.

"If it is alright with you, will you come with me?" Nephteros recalled the girl who held out her hand to her as she said those warm words, then shook her head to clear out the memory.

I was the one who chose not to join her…

Did she not choose to stay under Bifrons' service?

"I'll… come again," Nephteros curtly replied, affirming her resolve as she walked away.

After reaching the entrance hall, she strolled out toward the grounds. On the way, she passed by several sorcerers, but unlike before, none of them were the least bit hostile. It seemed they recognized Nephteros as a guest now.

Taking a fleeting glimpse behind her, Nephteros spotted Raphael waving his hand to her with a stern expression on his face. And she unintentionally waved back at him.

What exactly am I doing here...? Nephteros was unable to explain her own actions, but oddly enough, that didn't feel bad. And as she tried to leave the peaceful atmosphere of Zagan's castle that she had gotten completely absorbed in, another sorcerer came flying toward her from the forest.

"Shit, shit! That asshole Zagan's leaving me out of the fun stuff again! Why am I the one stuck with protecting that crybaby? Dammit!"

What's with this punk...?

He looked to be around twenty years old, with unkempt hair and large shadows under his eyes. He was a skinny and tall figure with gaunt cheeks that gave off an unhealthy impression. There were also many ornaments hanging around his neck, and they jingled about as he walked. She believed he was a sorcerer, but Nephteros did not know him.

That man was Barbatos. As a matter of fact, Nephteros had actually met him once, but things were so hectic back then that she didn't remember him at all. In an attempt to keep from getting involved with him, she walked off of the path. However, Barbatos simply stared at her fixedly.

"Huh? Wait, aren't you that elf from Bifrons' ball!?"

"...Who are you?" Nephteros knit her brows, but the man didn't pay that any mind and began talking to her.

"What's this? Did you come to kill that asshole Zagan? Well, too bad! That jerk ran off somewhere with his bride again. Kah! Looks like you wasted your time coming here, huh?"

"No, that's not really true…"

The cookies and tea were both delicious, and she even ended up being given a souvenir. Frankly, she was glad to have a reason to come again.

Unfortunately, Barbatos just kept chattering on, and as Nephteros began walking again in an attempt to escape him, he just followed along.

What's with this guy?

"If you're looking for Zagan, it seems he went to Nephelia's hometown. Why not deliver any complaints you have yourself?" Nephteros snapped at him after a while in order to drive him off.

She felt bad about forcing such an annoying man onto Zagan, but she could not endure his prattling any longer.

"What's that? By Nephy's hometown, you mean the hidden elven village, right? I see… He's going that far just to get his hands on a new power, huh? That's why he left me behind!" Barbatos exclaimed, his eyes shooting wide open as he took in Nephteros' words.

Nephteros hurriedly distanced herself from him as he repeatedly stamped his foot into the ground.

With this, I can finally return home… Nephteros felt a sense of relief at last, but Barbatos ended up ruining that by saying something completely unpredictable.

"I'm going after that asshole Zagan. You're planning to do the same, right? I'll take you with me, then."

"No, I'm not really…"

"Damn, that means I need to bring the crybaby along, too. Man, what a pain."

At that moment, Nephteros finally realized one of her faults. *Now that I think of it, I don't know how to deal with people who don't listen to others at all.*

Her master, Bifrons, was one good example, and this man was another. She never had the opportunity to strike up a conversation with people other than Bifrons, so that flaw made sense.

Sadly, that weakness was coming back to bite her now. Despite her objections, she ended up getting dragged into Barbatos' little expedition.

And just like that, Nephy's dark counterpart ended up hot on her trail, running headfirst into a situation that had absolutely nothing to do with her.

"W-Wait just a moment. Falling... I'm falling!" Gremory screamed in a hoarse voice. Ever since this morning, she had taken on the form of an old woman.

Zagan and the others were currently riding on the back of a dragon, soaring through the sky. The scenery beneath them changed with the flow of the clouds. Right as they saw a forest spreading out below, in an instant, a desert would appear, and next, a magnificent canal.

"Are you alright, Miss Gremory?" Nephy called out to the old woman in a worried voice.

"Keeheehee, you elves are such kindhearted creatures! Mmm, how comforting. I'm alright... Ah, sorry, no, maybe I'm not."

Zagan let out a sigh, resigning himself to his fate, as he grabbed the old woman who looked to be on the verge of fainting by the nape of her neck and pulled her back up.

The beautiful green dragon turned her head and pointed her amber eyes to those on her back.

"Should I... slow down a bit?" Foll's voice rang out. This green dragon with feathers similar to those of a bird was Foll's original form. She still had a petite figure for a dragon, but even so, her body was far larger than a carriage, and when she spread out her wings, she was about as large as a cabin.

A lion running through the sky drew near the tip of Foll's nose. It was Kimaris.

"No, it's alright. Miss Gremory is just bad with heights. Even if you change your speed, she'll just say the same thing," he said.

"That so?" Foll said, then faced forward as if having lost any concern for the old woman. After that, she picked up her pace.

"Eeeeeeeeeeeeeeeek!"

"If you were going to kick up a fuss, then you should have just obediently ridden on Kimaris' back," Zagan said, grimacing at the old woman screaming right next to his ear.

Zagan was at the center of Foll's back, Nephy was to his left, and Gremory to his right. Though, since Gremory had given up on staying stable with her own strength, Zagan was holding her up by the nape of her neck. Add in Foll and Kimaris, and there were five of them on the trip.

Zagan had imagined this as a family trip with his bride and daughter, but Gremory had grumbled until he was forced to take her along. Thanks to her, Kimaris ended up joining them, as well.

"That's unreasonable, Sir Zagan. Sure, I'm confident in my speed, but only when I'm on my own. Lady Foll's ability to transport passengers far surpasses mine."

Foll's flight speed was astounding. What would normally take a horse-drawn carriage three days only took her an evening. It seemed the only race that could fly at such high speeds while carrying people were dragons.

"Well, I get that much, but wouldn't it be better if she took on a younger form?" Zagan questioned.

It seemed she was shaking like a leaf in the wind in her old form. Even if sorcerers could manipulate physical abilities, an aging

body still took its toll. It was obvious that a younger body contained more power.

"This form is the lightest, you hear!? An old woman has more power than a young girl, you hear!? If I'm heavier, then flying would just be harder!" Gremory glared at Zagan, seemingly on the verge of tears as she said that.

"I'll fly… a little slower."

Well, setting aside whether an old woman had more power than a young girl, Gremory seemed to be trying to lighten Foll's load in her own little way. Once that became apparent, Foll consciously slowed herself down.

"Why are you so desperate to tag along with us…?" Zagan asked in a bewildered tone.

"Keehee, why do you think I'm following and serving you? Is it not obviously because as long as I'm in your service, I can observe dragons and elves all I want? If these two are going, then there's no meaning in just waiting behin— Eeeeeek!?"

Gremory was a sorcerer who researched the simple yet difficult to understand nature of immortality, so it was only natural that she had her eyes on races like elves and dragons, who possessed perpetual youth. And it seemed she came along to observe Nephy and Foll.

Well, I'm the same, in a way. I need to live a long life.

A normal human's lifespan was far too short. If Zagan wished to grow old with Nephy and Foll, he needed to lengthen it significantly. In that way, Gremory's research was a huge boon for him. As such, Zagan had no intention of mistreating Gremory. However…

"Well, when it comes to loving them, I will admit that you're quite skilled. Still, from my point of view, you have a long way to go.

Contrary to the great power possessed by elves and dragons, humans are delicate beings, therefore—"

What does she mean by "skilled," exactly...? Zagan pointed an exasperated gaze at her while she was talking, and perhaps having noticed that, Gremory glared back at him.

"What's that? Looks like you have something to say, my dear Archdemon."

"Who knows..." Zagan shrugged his shoulders in response, and contrary to expectations, Gremory returned a serious expression to him.

"Hear me, my liege, for these are the words of my mentor. If you desire immortality, then you will lose your 'love power,' you know?"

"L-Love... what?" Zagan had never heard the words put together like that, so he doubted his ears.

"I said love power. We sorcerers possess perpetual youth already. If we aim beyond that, and seek true immortality, then no matter how devoted to our research we become, we will eventually be tormented by boredom. And when that happens, the utopia that we sought will turn into an eternal prison."

Zagan was unable to simply laugh off those words, as they seemed to ring true. And, after a short pause, Gremory continued her speech.

"The only thing that can cure a person's loneliness when that comes to pass is being able to love something other than themselves. Look at the Archdemons we have now. It's because they possess no love power that they rush into foolish acts like Bifrons. And due to that, his elf is helplessly pitiable."

Despite how vague that sounded, Zagan was unable to deny what she was saying.

"…It seems most people won't die from being alone, but they are also unable to live happily."

Those were the words said to him back when he selfishly tried to keep Nephy at a distance. And as he repeated them to Gremory, Nephy's ears quivered shyly.

"So you remember that, Master Zagan."

"Of course. Do you think I would ever dare forget the words we exchange?"

Nephy said that she wanted to be by his side even after he abandoned her. And back then, he truly believed he had been saved from eternal solitude by her words. Thanks to that, even Zagan understood people were unable to live alone. Sure, a person could protect themselves, but they were unable to live a fulfilling life on their own.

"That's embarrassing…" Nephy wanted to bury her face in her hands, but they were on the back of a dragon. So, since she had to hold Foll tight, she buried her face in Zagan's mantle instead.

"Mmm, nice love power!" Gremory remarked, nodding as if praising Zagan as she did so.

…I really would have liked the three of us to just go as a family.

The old woman was noisy and annoying, but he still couldn't bring himself to kick her off midair.

And just like that, the group traveled until night began to fall, at which point a snow-covered mountain range came into view.

"We're almost there. Once we pass over those mountains, we'll be in Norden."

It was a place filled with miserable memories of Nephy's childhood. And yet, they continued on their way to the place she was raised.

A dark forest spread out before the group after they crossed over the snowy mountains. It wasn't as eerie as the one surrounding Zagan's castle, but the darkness was because the forest was made up of conifers with dark leaves that were tightly packed together. Perhaps because of the high elevation, the mountain was covered in snow, but the trees still had leaves.

It was said that the hidden elven village was concealed within this forest. It couldn't be approached from the sky, so Zagan and the others were walking the rest of the way. Foll also returned to her form as a little girl... and was being given a piggyback ride by Zagan.

"...I'm tired."

"You held on well. Just get some sleep."

"Okay..." Foll was fast asleep within seconds.

It's only natural that she's this tired.

They had decided to travel to Nephy's hometown at noon yesterday. And after getting their preparations in order, they left early in the morning today, and now it was evening.

They took a few breaks along the way, but it was almost an entire day of continuous flight.

"Foll tried her best today, didn't she?" Nephy said as she snuggled up next to him.

"She did. It may be best to prepare a bed for her now. Finding your hometown can wait."

"My apologies. If I knew of its location, then we wouldn't have to spend all this time searching for it..." Nephy's ears drooped apologetically as she said that.

Due to her status as a cursed child, Nephy wasn't even permitted to leave the village, so she didn't really know the surroundings of her

village at all. That was why they had to carefully investigate the area from here on out.

"Nephy, you weren't even able to leave the village, right? Then just think of this as sightseeing. I'm actually quite interested in the area, so a stroll seems good to me," Zagan claimed as he shook his head like it was no big deal.

I really would like to take a look around...

Luckily, this time around, he managed to put it in a way that wasn't misleading. Nephy stared at him in surprise, but the tips of her pointy ears were quivering with a twitch in a somewhat happy manner as she walked next to him.

And just then, a large shadow was suddenly cast over them. It was Kimaris. He had returned to his humanoid form.

"Sir Zagan, I believe I can figure out the location of Lady Nephy's village."

"What, really?"

"Yes. It seems there isn't any sorcery in place to stall us, or perhaps it has already lost its function. Whatever the case, we should be able to get there by following Lady Nephy's scent."

Zagan nodded and sank into thought. The sky was already dyed red, so if even an hour were to pass, it would turn pitch black. If they spent too long moving about, Nephy would join Foll in the depths of slumber. Plus, Gremory was riding on Kimaris' back already, too.

"...That seems to be the best course of action. Well, I'm counting on you, Kimaris."

Zagan wanted to try wandering around, but getting to the hidden village earlier was the best option. Even if it was abandoned, having buildings to take shelter from the rain and wind would be a huge help.

"Please leave it to me," Kimaris responded, a smile creeping onto his face. He returned a small nod and began walking ahead of them, exuding a sense of reliability that made Zagan think of Raphael.

Nephy tightly gripped the hems of Zagan's robe as they walked. He took a fleeting glance back at her, and saw that the tips of her pointy ears were drooping.

"Are you anxious?"

"Yes. In truth, I'm just a little... scared. Of seeing the village as it is now, I mean," Nephy replied, her body trembling all the while.

In her own way, Nephy had come to terms with her past. However, this was still a village where she left people to die.

If Zagan was in her shoes, he would have laughed upon seeing its dilapidated state, but he didn't think Nephy would be able to imitate that... and honestly, he didn't want her to.

After thinking about it a little, Zagan adjusted Foll's position on his back so he was carrying her with one arm. Then, he took his now free hand, gripped one of Nephy's, and gave it a tight squeeze.

"Ah..." Nephy's expression didn't change, but the tips of her pointy ears stood up stiffly.

Now I just need to say something to ease her mind... Unfortunately, that was the hardest possible task for him. Zagan had still not even said 'I love you' to Nephy, so there was no chance of him saying anything heartwarming in this situation.

Nevertheless, remaining silent was unacceptable in Zagan's mind. Maybe he was being guided by 'love power,' as Gremory put it.

"You may rely on me to your heart's content. I find it quite amusing," Zagan proclaimed.

Wait, amusing? Doesn't that make it sound like I'm delighted by Nephy's suffering?

"I will!" Nephy answered, nodding as if she understood him completely. She may have just been putting up a strong front, but Nephy at least seemed a little more energetic as she spoke.

"...Sir Zagan, it seems we'll be arriving at our destination shortly," Kimaris declared in a voice rife with tension.

Upon looking forward, Zagan spotted the red light of sundown pouring in through a break in the dense forest. When they looked down from the skies, they didn't spot anything like a gap in the trees, yet there was still somehow an open space in front of them.

In spite of their fortuitous discovery, Kimaris' voice contained no relief or joy. Instead, it was filled to the brim with apprehension. After a moment of hesitation, Gremory climbed off Kimaris' back and gripped her large scythe in hand.

"Is something there?" Nephy asked.

"Seems like it," Zagan answered. He could tell Nephy poured all her strength into gripping his hand. The hidden village was once the target of Archdemon Marchosias, who held the second name Eldest, and it was also assaulted by Archdemon Bifrons in a bid to capture Nephy. In other words, Nephy's hometown was already involved with two different Archdemons.

Worst of all, no one in Zagan's group knew of what had actually transpired. They had no clue what cruel, repulsive things the two Archdemons had done. Now that they'd made it so far, though, they knew things wouldn't go smoothly any longer. After all, the Archdemons' influence could have lingered...

"Let's go," Zagan said in order to spur on his subordinates. Then, he walked forth into the light. And the sight he took in once his eyes adjusted was rather shocking...

"Oh, well if it ain't Zagan. You're late, man. We got tired of waiting and emptied out a bottle already, buddy."

For some reason, his undesirable friend was brazenly drinking some liquor alongside two women.

$$\Diamond$$

"What the hell are you doing here?" Zagan was stunned by the sight before him.

There were three people surrounding a bonfire in Nephy's hometown. Zagan's group couldn't tell it was there because of the sunlight, but they even had some soup boiling over it.

However, the only one in good humor was Barbatos. The other two seemed to be on the verge of tears. It was a terrible atmosphere.

Zagan took a look around at the village. Unlike Kianoides, there were only a few dozen houses which seemed to be built into natural rock formations. The roofs were all woven out of straw. In the center of the village, there was an open plaza and a decrepit well.

Zagan had heard Bifrons had this place attacked, but contrary to expectations, the buildings were left in a clean state. There were a few that had been burned down, but the place looked otherwise untouched.

He assumed it would have more of a sacred atmosphere, but it actually felt just like a normal village.

I wonder where Nephy lived? Zagan knew that was probably something Nephy didn't wish to recall, but he still looked about restlessly in anticipation.

"Well, you know, you just went and left me behind again, so I thought maybe I'd deliver a nice surprise. Heeheeheeheeheeee!" Barbatos took a swig of his drink and laughed, clearly in good spirits.

51

"...How did you get here ahead of us?"

"Come on, did you forget my second name? Purgatory can reach anywhere, so all I had to do was dive in a teensy bit and look around. Gahahahaha!"

I really want to slug this damn drunk... Zagan had prepared himself to do battle with another Archdemon, but Barbatos was just fooling around without a care in the world.

Unable to resist the temptation, Zagan swung his fist at him. However, Nephy rushed over to stop him in a panic.

"Snap out of it, Master Zagan! If you don't stop, Sir Barbatos will die!"

"...Ah, sorry, I started punching on reflex."

The phrase 'my body moved before I even knew it,' surely referred to just such situations. Zagan grabbed Barbatos by his collar and drove his fist into his face unconsciously. From the wounds he could see, it appeared he had punched Barbatos a good ten times. Barbatos' eyes were completely peeled back as his head swayed in circles.

Zagan threw aside his foolish friend like a sack of garbage when a girl came running over to them.

"Nephy, are you alright? I heard you were going through something terrible in your hometown, uh... Huh? Wait, did you... just get here now?"

The girl was wearing Anointed Armor. She had her beautiful red hair, which resembled polished copper, tied to the side, and her scarlet eyes were filled with tears. Her shapely, toned body was pleasing to the eye, and her appearance was well in order, but it was all ruined by how she quickly broke down into tears whenever they met.

She was the lone woman among the Archangels who wielded Sacred Swords, Crybaby Knight Chastille.

She's not a bad person, but... At any rate, she was a girl whose disappointing features always stood out most.

"I-I'm alright, Chastille."

"No way... Did I misunderstand the situation again!?" Chastille placed her hand on her chest in relief upon verifying Nephy's safety, but then immediately formed an awkward expression on her face.

"That is not the case. Meeting you here has me feeling a little relieved."

Makes sense. Seeing someone more shaken up than you is bound to make you feel better... Surely Nephy wasn't looking at Chastille in the same way as Zagan, but there was something that oozed out of her that spurred on one's sadistic tendencies.

"Mmm...?" Foll opened her eyes as she let out that noise. Her wandering gaze stopped on Nephy and Chastille holding hands, which made her speak in a dazed voice.

"I can see Horse Head... Did I... die?"

"Why would you be dead because I'm here!? Just so you know, I'm still alive and kicking!"

"What... so this is all a dream?" Foll fell asleep once more, seemingly relieved by her revelation.

Zagan tilted his head to the side upon seeing Chastille on the verge of tears due to her humiliation, then questioned her.

"Tell me, why'd you even come here?"

"That's, um... That man was kicking up a fuss, saying Nephy was in distress, and that girl was with him, so I assumed it was something important..." Chastille mumbled in response.

The words 'that girl' made Zagan shift his attention to the girl who was hugging her knees as she warmed herself by the fire.

"Well, this is pretty standard behavior for Chastille, but—"

"Hold on, what's that supposed to mean!? Ah, but it's been a while since you've called me by my name..." Chastille's teary face turned a little red as she said that, but Zagan pretended not to notice and continued questioning her.

"Look, I'm saying I get why you're here, but what about Bifrons' subordinate?"

"Please leave me alone. This time around, I really didn't have any intent to mess with all of you," Nephteros said in a voice filled with self-loathing.

Where had the high-handed attitude she had the last time they met gone? Right now, she was cradling her knees like a starving orphan and her eyes looked vacant. She didn't appear to be scared, but Zagan could tell that she was feeling down.

"She's been like that since they came over to my place. Seems she went through something painful... Well, at the very least, she doesn't look to be hostile, so can you try to cheer her up?" Chastille whispered to Zagan and Nephy.

"What exactly do you expect me to do?" Zagan was terrible at speaking to people, and Nephy was much the same. There was no way either of them could cheer her up.

"Um, Miss Nephteros…" Nephy tried calling out to her first, but Gremory stopped her.

"Hold on a bit. I shall show you the essence of love power here and now," Gremory proclaimed as she took a seat next to Nephteros.

"Keeheehee, have you had an unpleasant experience recently…? I suppose it's fine if you don't wish to speak of it. More importantly, how about you try some candy? If you eat something sweet, you'll feel more at ease!" Gremory claimed as she pulled a bag of sweets out of nowhere. There were many chocolate balls packed together inside.

They were most likely leftovers from the sweets she made the previous day.

"Now that I think of it, wasn't there a story about an old woman tricking a girl into eating a poisoned apple?" Zagan asked as a sense of apprehension overtook him.

"You're thinking of 'Snow White and the Seven Dwarves,' I believe. Long ago, I saw it in a picture book someone left around. Though, I was mistaken for a thief soon after."

"I see. We've finally made it back to your hometown, Nephy. It may be fun to resurrect the fools who dared to do such things and force them to atone, don't you think?" Zagan nodded at his own idea.

"Calling somebody out of their grave over something so trivial is a bit much… Putting that aside, Master Zagan, I'm surprised you're aware of such a story," Nephy said, her ears quivering to emphasize her point.

"Sure, the apple was poisoned, but a tale of a girl filling her belly, then getting rich by sleeping was something I envied back then."

"You have a point. Even if it was poisoned, it's only natural to eat whatever food is given to you."

"Quit being so noisy! All those sad stories are making my heart hurt!" Gremory yelled at them in a tone that was a mix of anger and sympathy.

Despite the rather odd conversation, Nephteros was their real focus, and they could clearly see the tips of her long ears jump as she gazed at the chocolate. She was still staring at the bonfire with a hollow gaze, but it was obvious she was interested in the sweets.

Do the ears of all elves move based on their emotions? If that really was the case, then Zagan was glad they were so easy to understand.

Gremory stuck out her bag of chocolate with a smile on her face. Nephteros had surely heard what Zagan and the others were talking about mere moments ago, yet her hand still stuck out to take a piece of chocolate. Perhaps her mental state was on the brink of collapse.

This looks exactly like a girl being tricked by a shady old woman... Gremory herself was most definitely a suspicious sorcerer, so there was no other way to interpret the situation.

"...Didn't I say to just leave me alone?" Nephteros didn't even look at the old woman as she muttered those words.

"Keeheehee, I can do no such thing when a young woman makes such a pained expression before me. How about it? There's no poison in here, I swear!" Gremory made a show of throwing a chocolate into her mouth.

Seeing that the old woman wouldn't budge an inch, Nephteros raised her face to speak.

"...After I eat this, you'll leave me alone, right?" she said as she reluctantly put a chocolate ball in her mouth.

"It's sweet…" Nephteros uttered, her golden eyes blinking in surprise.

"Of course it is! How about another?"

"Mmm…" Nephteros pushed the chocolate into her cheek with a completely dejected face.

…Is she really alright? Seeing her depressed state even spurred on Zagan's protective instinct. Plus, both Nephy and Chastille donned tense expressions.

"H-Hold on! Didn't I tell you to leave me alone!?" Nephteros screamed. Seemed she'd finally returned to her senses after gobbling down a bunch of Gremory's chocolates.

"Sure looks like you're full of energy now," Gremory said, nodding with a satisfied look on her face as she handed Nephteros the entire bag of chocolates.

"Jeez…" Nephteros groaned in irritation, but she didn't throw away the bundle.

Doesn't that mean she's recovered in her own little way?

The dark elf continued to grumble her complaints as she corrected her posture in front of the bonfire. The fact that she wanted to be left alone didn't change, and she still wasn't looking in the direction of Zagan's group, but unlike before, she wasn't huddled up with vacant eyes.

"Now then, what do you think?" Gremory inquired as she returned to Zagan's side.

"How do you expect me to answer that question?" Yeah, she did succeed in cheering up Nephteros, but Zagan had no clue how love power factored in to her actions.

"Zagan also… baited me with food once. Nephy's soup… was really delicious," Foll murmured, then began squirming around on Zagan's back.

Do you really have to bring that up? When Foll first entered his castle, Zagan gave her some soup, which tempted her into staying with him. Saying that she was baited with food was completely accurate, but he didn't really want to admit it.

Zagan casually looked over at Nephteros in an attempt to distract himself, then noticed the girl's ears start to tremble.

I guess she's irritated that we think she was tempted by food. She can't really get angry, though, since that'd be the same as admitting it... Zagan found that she had an unexpectedly charming side to her as he continued to gaze at her.

"Keeheehee, as I'd expect of the Archdemon I've placed my hopes in. Techniques of this caliber are simply natural to you, I see," Gremory said with a satisfied laugh.

"What does baiting people with food have to do with loving them?"

Nephteros' ears began twitching about again, but Zagan paid them no mind. He knew he could just treat her to some of Nephy's soup later to make up for things.

"Did I not say that I would show you the essence of love power?" Gremory said, then pointed to Nephteros and continued, "If one eats their fill, then they'll be able to put their heart at ease. That's what I did, but even without love power, anybody could accomplish that."

"Well, that's true..." Zagan did the same thing for Foll, after all. Eventually, he returned a nod, which made Gremory thrust her finger at him repeatedly.

"Then answer this. When you saw such a crabby little girl gingerly taking candy from me, what did you feel?" Gremory asked, then slowly sidled up next to Zagan and whispered in his ear like a devil, "You felt charmed, correct?"

"Erk…" Zagan's body stiffened up as he realized Gremory had seen right through him.

"What did you think when her eyes shot open due to the sweetness of the chocolate? How about when she bashfully muttered 'It's sweet…?' And then, at the end, how about the way she tried to hide her embarrassment with a 'Jeez…?'"

She shot out each and every word as if trying to stab Zagan. And the stray fire from them slammed right into Nephteros, leading her to bite down on her lips and let out bitter groans. Seeing her react like that, Gremory's lips curved into a grand smile.

"'She has an unexpected cute side…' I'm sure that thought came to mind."

"Ugh, I didn't really feel—"

"It's fine," Gremory claimed, cutting him off and continuing with, "That's just it, my Archdemon. When you see something adorable, you feel relaxed, don't you? Would anyone take offense to loving the look of a bunny scratching its head? Is it strange to be fascinated by the sight of a beautiful flower? However, wanting to love such things for your entire life is an entirely different matter.

"Hear me, Archdemon, love all creation. If you do, the world itself shall become yours!" Gremory spread her arms wide and yelled.

There was something about her words that Zagan couldn't just laugh off as nonsense.

"Hear me, Archdemon. If you feel love, a flower on the roadside will become a treasure that surpasses even a mountain of gold. The ability to accumulate such treasures… is love power!" Gremory proclaimed with a suspicious grin on her face.

Zagan couldn't understand a single thing she was saying, but she was speaking with such fervor that it felt she was unraveling a fundamental truth of the world.

"Then, Miss Gremory, by some chance… is it the same as the throbbing I feel in my chest when I see Master Zagan worry so much about saying just a single phrase correctly?" Nephy asked, clearly taken aback by Gremory's explanation.

That's way too specific! How does she know me so well? Zagan covered his face, barely managing to keep from passing out.

On the other hand, Gremory stared at her in wonder before responding.

"Amazing! To think the Archdemon is loved… No, of course he is! You are fit to be by his side because you love him. So I dare to say… Nice love power!"

Next, while squirming on Zagan's back, Foll raised her hand.

"Then, the soothing feeling I get when I see Zagan put Nephy on his lap and squeeze her tight is the same?"

"Indeed! And the way that butler refuses to show that to you and covers your face is also some splendid love power."

Nephy covered her face and squatted down after being hit with an unexpected counterattack.

"You already get it, don't you? The act of comforting a pitiful lass is not love power, but drawing out her charm and perceiving it as adorable is. You have both the talent and the power for it. One day, you will surely ascend to heights even beyond me," Gremory whispered to Zagan with a satisfied look on her face.

Zagan could only groan as she praised him for something he didn't want anything to do with.

If she became an Archdemon instead of me, wouldn't the world have gotten totally messed up? He started regretting that such a sorcerer was under his command, but at the same time, he knew it would have been worse if she was left at large.

61

At that point, Nephteros finally seemed to have run out of patience as she stood up.

"You, the fomorian over there, I've been quietly listening for a while now, but you sure have some nerve. Cut it out alread— Eeek?" Nephteros was trying to pressure her to stop, but she suddenly let out a scream instead. Zagan looked up to see what was going on, and before he knew it, Gremory had transformed from an old woman to a young, beautiful one. Then, in that form, she started gently caressing Nephteros.

They two of them looked odd together. Nephteros seemed to have fallen backward, and Gremory embraced her from behind and ran her finger along Nephteros' chin.

"Keehee, your angry face is also quite lovely, isn't it? Do not pleasure me in such ways. I'll lose my patience!"

"Eeek, wh-what are you…"

"Oh my, your skin is beautiful. Your golden eyes and white hair are also splendid. Keehee, come now, is this really enough to make you blush?"

"S-Stop… Let me… Oh…"

When it came to simple power as a sorcerer, Nephteros should have been far superior, but having such straightforward words of praise showered on her made her go limp. Her dark skin was tinted bright red, and the way her hand was trembling in anxiety atop her chest made her seem like a nervous little girl.

"L-Let me go… I'm… telling you… to let me… go…"

"Keeheehee, you truly are quite innocent, aren't you? Well, if you're set on teasing me, then I'll guide you. Go on, call me 'sister dearest.'"

In that moment, Zagan recalled that Gremory held the second name Enchantress.

Nephteros was grimacing at the humiliation of it all, but her disagreeable attitude eventually turned to quivers of defeat. And then, just as she was opening her mouth to signal that she'd succumbed…

"Ow!" Kimaris mercilessly smacked Gremory's head.

"Miss Gremory, please restrain yourself."

"You son of a… Don't get in my way, Kimaris! Just a bit more and this girl would have been unable to live without me!"

Why did I bring someone like her with me again…? Oh, right, she just invited herself.

After watching such misleading conduct, Zagan was once more reminded just how loyal and capable Raphael was.

With Gremory's attention drawn away, Nephteros was liberated from her arms. However, since she'd completely lost all strength in her legs, it didn't seem like she could stand.

"I must apologize to you as well, Miss Nephteros. Once she becomes like this, it's hard to control her…" Kimaris apologized to her on Gremory's behalf as he caught her in his fluffy arm. After steadying her, Kimaris let Nephteros down, then grabbed Gremory by the back of her neck and lifted her up.

Nephteros used that opening to distance herself from Gremory and hide behind Zagan. She even scurried across the ground on all fours to get away as fast as possible. Frankly, the sight was quite pitiful. Feeling bad about it, Zagan opened his mouth to speak.

"Ah… Sorry that the old hag messed with you."

"No… It seems like you've been through a lot as well, Archdemon Zagan."

"It isn't normally like this, I swear…" Nephy responded to Nephteros in a weary voice. In that moment, a strange sense of camaraderie was born between the three of them.

On the other hand, Gremory and Kimaris were still going at each other.

"Leeet meee gooo!"

"I will, so please help me make dinner. The sun has already set, and it's pitch dark out here."

The sun had set while Gremory was screwing around. At his words, everyone came to the conclusion that it was time to start pitching tents and cooking dinner, but Chastille raised her voice in a fluster to stop them.

"H-Hold on, Barbatos has stopped moving completely!"

Zagan thought the two of them were strangely quiet, so that made sense. Chastille was tending to Barbatos, who still hadn't woken up. The sight made Zagan suddenly recall a certain doubt he had in mind.

"I don't really care about Barbatos, but is it alright not to show some love to that one?" Zagan asked Gremory.

"Where's the fun in showing love to a crybaby who's favored by everyone with little effort? Besides, do you really think I'd ever love an Angelic Knight?"

Chastille was left speechless by those harsh words.

Zagan's group chose to sleep in a particularly large house that was still standing. The silver furnishings made it readily apparent that some sort of noble once lived there. Having said that, the construction of the house itself was the same as the other houses,

and though the floor was composed of wooden boards, the walls were simply made of rocks piled atop one another. Moss was growing rampantly along them, making it feel like they were staying in a cave. Still, including the basement, there were enough rooms for over ten people, so that was good enough for them.

Zagan held his hand up to a silver candlestick on the wall, then gathered his mana and lit it. It was a fundamental power that couldn't even really be called sorcery.

"So this… is the house of the chief of those elves… is it?" Zagan muttered as he gazed down the now-colorful corridor.

"Yes. This is the elder's manor. Though… this is the first time I've been here…" Nephy nodded as she replied to Zagan's question.

That makes this the best place to look for any clues on celestial mysticism or high elves. Unfortunately, they had wasted all their sunlight thanks to Gremory, so they had to wait to search outside. Left with no other choice, Zagan, Nephy, Chastille, and Nephteros wandered through the house slowly.

"Why am I even here…" Nephteros let out some dissatisfied words. She had gotten dragged into this and had no way to return home on her own. Because of that, she was reluctantly cooperating with Zagan.

"You can just wait in the kitchen with Foll if you'd prefer."

To take responsibility for the earlier uproar, Gremory and Kimaris agreed to take care of dinner. Foll was taking a break in the kitchen, chowing down on some snacks while waiting. And since Barbatos wasn't waking up, they just threw him in the first room they could find and left him to rot.

"No, it's not like this is all bad. Besides, it would be boring to just sit around and do nothing," Nephteros replied, trembling in response to Zagan's question. It seemed the terror of Gremory

messing around with her wasn't so easily forgotten. Honestly, it felt like she was actually saying 'for the love of god, anywhere but the kitchen.'

"Well, relax. Sure, Bifrons gets on my nerves, but I'm not going to hold that against you. I'll look after you until we get back," Zagan said, shrugging his shoulders.

Barbatos was at fault for her current predicament, but as an Archdemon, Zagan thought it best to at least be a little generous.

"About Master Bifrons... Um..." Nephteros' dark ears quivered as she hung her head.

Zagan was unable to catch what she said beyond her initial words. He tilted his head to the side in confusion, intending to ask her to speak up, but Chastille spoke first.

"What a strange building. It feels like the aura of my Sacred Sword is sharpening from just being here..." Chastille said as she touched the walls around her.

"You sure about that?" Zagan's eyes widened upon hearing something so unexpected.

"It seems like Norden really might be sacred land. Even the church's cathedrals are nowhere near as spiritually clean..." Chastille claimed, sticking her chest out in pride. It seemed that the energy Sacred Swords possessed that was similar to mana was called 'aura.'

"I'm sure I'll be able to draw out the true power of my Sacred Sword in this place. And this time around, I'm wearing my Anointed Armor, so I won't be scared by any enemy!" Chastille proclaimed, nodding repeatedly in admiration of the place the entire time.

"Wouldn't the most likely enemies in this place be the ghosts of the elves whose beds we're using?"

"Eeek, ghosts!?" Chastille shrieked, turning completely pale in a flash.

"I really hope this isn't true... but... are you scared of ghosts?" Zagan asked in an exasperated voice.

"I-I mean, come on, they're dead people who just pop up out of nowhere!"

"Isn't dealing with ghosts and the undead a part of your job as an Angelic Knight?"

The church didn't only do battle with sorcerers. It was also their job to respond to the concerns and grievances of their followers. And since sorcerers often enslaved ghosts and the undead, Angelic Knights had to go fight them.

For an Archangel of all people to be scared of ghosts... How pathetic. Chastille was unable to hide her trembling hands as she replied to his question.

"A job is a job, but scary things are scary. What's wrong with that?"

Even Nephteros was let down by that response.

"...Do you not even possess a notion of self-respect or pride?" Zagan asked.

"I believe that being too proud is a recipe for disaster."

Well, that sure fit her meek, crybaby persona. In truth, Zagan was genuinely curious how such a person ever even became an Angelic Knight.

Oh, right, she was chosen by her Sacred Sword. Her sense of responsibility was strong, so she was probably unable to free herself from her burden against better judgment. Perhaps Gremory had said there was 'no need to show any love' to her because of her strong convictions.

"I-Is that so...?" Nephteros faltered in her response. It seemed Chastille's rather dignified response had stumped her. Her tone

made it apparent that she was unsure whether to sympathize with her point of view or scorn her for it.

This girl... Looks like she's bad at dealing with unexpected responses, huh? Thinking back on it, she was quite shaken when Zagan wasn't tricked at all by her Nephy act. After taking that into consideration, Zagan was sure her arrogant attitude was all an act. And with that in mind, it was clear that Nephteros was quite loveable.

This is bad. I've started thinking of love far too much thanks to Gremory. She was truly terrifying. Gremory had even managed to infect the ever-apathetic Zagan...

"Now that I think of it, it seems like you can't really handle Foll either, can you?" Zagan muttered to Chastille as he pulled himself together.

"I-It's not like I hate her or anything, okay? It's just, every time I meet her, she pulls some kind of prank on me..."

"But her second name is Apparition..."

"Eeek!"

When Foll went by Valefor, she wore armor fit for a giant. Due to her short stature, the interior was largely vacant, which helped her earn her second name.

"I see... That's why she's so good at targeting my weaknesses..." Chastille said as she turned pale and began trembling.

Maybe it would've been better not to mention it... For the time being, Zagan decided to watch Chastille carefully as he continued to check out the state of the house.

"It doesn't seem like there are any traps made with sorcery here."

Elves avoided conflict when possible, but each of them possessed an extraordinary amount of mana. That was why Zagan assumed they set up traps to protect themselves and their secrets. However, oddly enough, he failed to locate anything of the sort.

"I never once saw the people of my village use sorcery. Perhaps I'm wrong, and they were just hiding it from me, but I don't think anyone knew how," Nephy said with downcast eyes.

Aside from sorcery, there was also the power of mysticism, but only high elves like Nephy and Nephteros could wield it.

"Really? But how did they defend themselves? It's not like they could've just avoided all monsters in this place."

Monsters were living creatures who possessed mana and differed greatly in appearance from people and animals. Among them, there were some who could even understand human speech, and it was rumored that those ones were closely related to demons. However, all they possessed was an impulse for destruction and hunger, so there was no way to ever talk them down.

Their population had grown thin around Kianoides, but monsters naturally attacked everything around them, and elves were no exception. It was said that such beings populated even the parts of Norden humans couldn't reach.

Instead of answering this, Nephy simply opened a nearby door. It seemed that it led to a parlor with a large table surrounded by rock seats. Unfortunately, all of the seats were now covered in moss. It was obviously not a storehouse, but it still stank of mud. And upon closer inspection, the smell wasn't all that surprising, as the stone seats were sticking out of the ground. It seemed the stones had been buried straight into the ground.

This was a type of barrier... Or well, it may have been a means of building up the spiritual aura Chastille had mentioned.

Lizards were creeping about the gaps in the floorboards. Even Zagan, whose castle was once filled with torture devices and skeletons, found it hard to believe people actually once lived there. And on a wall in that room... was a single bow.

"Everyone used a bow like this when it was time to hunt," Nephy said as she picked up the bow.

Zagan let out a 'Hm' in admiration as he gave it a once-over. The bow's main body was made of wood, but it had been elaborately decorated with silver ornaments. It appeared to be quite valuable, but...

"Those symbols are Celestian, aren't they?" Zagan spotted crests similar to those on a Sacred Sword on the bow.

"Yes. I don't quite understand what it means, but it says Exousiai..." Nephy replied with a nod.

"It means 'Evil's bane.' It's a charm that wards off evil spirits," Nephteros chimed in on their discussion.

"...You're going to help us?" Zagan inquired, clearly confused. "Are you sure it's fine for you to tell us?"

"...It's not like Master Bifrons gave me an order to keep quiet. Also, you're going to head back as soon as you finish investigating this place, right? In that case, I'll get home faster if I assist you," Nephteros claimed arrogantly. However, her twitching and swaying ears gave her true intentions away.

This girl's awfully easy to understand...

"Is something the matter?" Nephteros glared back at Zagan in response to his observant gaze.

"Well, it just seems like I'm the only one you're treating coldly. Don't you get tired of that?"

"Huh? Is that really the case?" Nephteros seemed unaware of her own behavior.

"Sure seemed like you were acting a lot more casual with Nephy and Gremory..."

"Perhaps you're right. I wasn't really conscious of it, though. It's just..."

"What?"

"You are... an Archdemon."

Did that mean she had to pay respect to him? Or perhaps it meant she feared him? For whatever reason, the thought bothered him.

"I'm not your master. I'm not saying to correct your tone, but you're a guest. There's no need to strain yourself when dealing with me... for now," Zagan remarked, shrugging his shoulders at her as he spoke. It was an entirely different matter when she was acting as Bifrons' servant, but at the moment, she was merely a guest who got dragged into Zagan's affairs. Given the circumstances, it was his responsibility to treat her well. And after he informed her of his thoughts on the matter, Nephteros relaxed a little.

"Underst... Got it. I'll talk a bit more casually, then."

"Sounds good to me."

Nephy's ears happily quivered as she heard their exchange. Seeing that, Nephteros glared back at her, barking out her next words.

"What? You got any complaints!?"

"Not at all! Thank you very much, Miss Nephteros. Having someone who understands Celestian is a big help. I'm relying on you."

"Th-That doesn't make me happy at all!" Nephteros denied feeling any sense of joy, but her twitching ears acted as a dead giveaway once more.

This kind of feels like a sibling rivalry or something... Nephteros had once tried to hurt Nephy, but Nephy had put that aside and was trying to accept her. Fighting and then making up afterward was textbook sibling rivalry. The sight made Zagan suddenly remember something.

"I want to save her. And then, I want to teach her as her senior..." When Nephteros was singing her celestial mysticism, her memories flowed into Zagan. That was why he knew that she didn't detest Nephy at all. In fact, she had even wanted to save Nephy after seeing how the people of her village treated her. Her current reactions made him think those feelings still resided within her. No, perhaps it was better to say those feelings had been reignited after all the time they spent together.

"This is likely a weapon built on the same concepts as a Sacred Sword... Though in comparison, it works a lot more like a toy. Simply drawing the string will allow anyone to fire off an arrow made of mana. Well, if they can actually use mana, anyway."

"I see. The bow itself must be an antique, then..." Zagan commented.

"I think you're right. This probably wasn't made by the residents of this village. I'd say it's from an age where high elves like myself and... this girl here were still common."

"Is it something valuable?" Nephy tilted her head to the side as she asked that question.

"I'd say the words 'legendary weapon' fit best. If the church got their hands on it, they'd probably enshrine it as a new sacred treasure or something."

"Uh, wouldn't that... put it on the same level as the Sacred Swords?" Chastille asked. Their discovery seemed to have stunned her.

"It's not quite on that level, but it's probably only a step below it. At the very least, it's far more powerful than your Anointed Armor."

Chastille's shoulders drooped down.

"Ugh, I finally came fully equipped and this happens..."

It made sense that a hidden elven village had such powerful artifacts lying around. In any case, Nephteros appeared to be quite proud of unraveling the mystery. Even the hostility she usually pointed toward Nephy had eased up.

Maybe I'm worrying too much... It may have been unreasonable at present, but perhaps the day would come where the two of them could spend time together happily.

After fixedly gazing at the bow for a while, Chastille let out a nod in admiration and spoke up.

"If I remember right, legends say elves are masters of the bow. They're a race who have a high amount of innate mana, so maybe this type of weapon suits them best."

"...Thanks for the explanation. Think you can keep a little further away from me, though?" Nephteros asked. Before anyone knew it, Chastille had started clinging to the hem of her mantle.

"B-But the room over there is so dark! I keep thinking something's going to pop out of there suddenly, so I just..."

"Are you really an Archangel? You're saying the church actually puts you on the same level as that butler?" Nephteros looked to be truly astonished by that fact. However, she didn't shake off Chastille's hand despite her rather evident disdain. Instead, she simply returned the bow to Nephy, then walked away.

"Tell me, how long do you plan on just standing around? We need to finish looking through all the rooms before the others finish preparing dinner, remember?"

"W-W-W-Wait up!"

Nephteros walked ahead of the group with Chastille still clinging to her.

Zagan and Nephy exchanged befuddled glances before following them with slightly bitter smiles on their faces.

"Even a run-down place like this has some nice liquor, huh?" Zagan let out a sigh of admiration as he knocked back some wine from a bottle he found in the cellar. It seemed to be quite well-aged wine, and its refined maturity danced about his tongue.

He was currently in one of the bedrooms in the village elder's manor. It was fairly empty, sporting only a plain side table next to a wooden bedframe and a small bookshelf with several handwritten books lining each row. After skimming through them, he quickly realized they were journals written in the language of elves.

The bed was packed with straw instead of cotton. Zagan tried taking a seat on it, and he found it quite pleasant. Usually, he slept on his throne, so actually sleeping on his back was a good change of pace. Moreover, this was the first time Nephy's room was completely separate from his, which allowed him to relax more. Back at the castle, Nephy's room was directly above the throne room. That meant she had to walk through the throne room to get to any of the common areas, so he had to be ready to meet her at any moment.

Zagan recalled what went on during dinner as he sat there and indulged in the wine. In the end, there were no traps in the manor that used sorcery or mysticism. After going back to reconvene with the rest of their group, the search party found dinner laid out for them in one of the larger rooms of the manor. The cooking team had managed to make a decent dinner out of whatever ingredients were left in the kitchen. However, since Foll decided to "help" with preparations, there was barely enough food left to fill everyone's bellies.

Gremory messed with Nephteros again as they ate. Zagan couldn't help but think she did it on purpose to ease Nephy's mind.

"Nephy… looked quite perplexed," Zagan said with a sigh as he gazed at the bright red liquid in his glass.

Her face… or rather, her ears told him that she didn't really know how to react, and that worried her far more than the state of her hometown. It appeared Gremory and Kimaris had caught on to her predicament as well. That was fairly surprising, as they'd only known her a short while.

Zagan was, of course, worried about her, but he knew asking someone if they were alright when they clearly weren't was irritating. Due to all that, their meal ended without Zagan even getting in a word. And after that, they all split up and went to rest in their rooms. For better or worse, the place had more than eight bedrooms, so everyone got their own.

Chastille, surprisingly, ended up taking dinner over to Barbatos. That undesirable friend of Zagan's had not woken up by the time dinner rolled around. Perhaps he had hit him a little too hard.

"That man may be utter trash, but he also has a good side that he shows once in a while. Sure, I'm stuck here because of his antics, but I got to meet you and Nephy and Zagan thanks to that," Chastille had said. Barbatos had been protecting Chastille on Zagan's command, so he had himself to blame, as well. Though, he was surprised that Chastille had stopped hating him.

Barbatos doesn't seem that bothered by it anymore, either… Well, all things considered, that was probably a good sign.

"More importantly, is Nephy…" Zagan finally had his own private room, but all he wanted to do was talk to her. Unfortunately, he didn't know what to say when Nephy was so clearly upset. Plus, there was also the fact that she probably wanted to be left alone, though what was the point of inviting him, in that case?

"...How ridiculous. I've got no reason to worry, right?" Zagan shook his head in an attempt to clear his mind after worrying over such thoughts for over half an hour. Then, he took the wine bottle in hand and stood up.

If I can't think of anything to say, I'll just stay by her side! Both Zagan and Nephy were terrible at putting their feelings into words. That was why they usually nestled up to each other when they were troubled. Why had he been hesitating when the answer was so obvious?

Oh, someone's here... He didn't realize it because he was lost in thought, but there was someone pacing restlessly in front of his door. After taking several steps to the right, they spun around and walked to the left. Zagan could tell that they had been repeating this cycle for quite some time now.

Nephy... No, those aren't her footsteps... Nephy always took great care to walk about silently, so Zagan would have known right away if that were her. Still, such light footsteps surely didn't belong to Kimaris or Barbatos either, which meant it was likely a woman. Having said that, they weren't light enough to be Foll's or loud enough to be Chastille's. Perhaps Gremory fit, as she could morph her body as she pleased, but she also wasn't very meek. In that case, the only remaining suspect was...

"What are you doing here... Nephteros!?"

"Erk?!" Nephteros stiffened up completely, a surprised look on her face, as Zagan swung his door open.

Seeing that expression on someone with the same face as Nephy is pretty refreshing... No matter what happened, Nephy would never make that kind of face. Nephteros' mouth was flapping open and shut for a while, as she was unable to say anything, but eventually, she brushed back her silver hair in an attempt to keep up appearances.

"I just happened to be passing by."

"Oh, that's nice…" Zagan decided to spare her dignity and let her lie slide. And though Nephteros averted her face from him in a huff, he could tell she had some business with him from the way she was casting him fleeting glances.

I want to head over to Nephy right away… Zagan wanted to be rid of Nephteros, but he had decided to treat her like a guest earlier, and a guest deserved some courtesy. Left with no other choice, Zagan tried to cut straight to the chase.

"Do you want something?"

"Um, well…" Nephteros winced and began to mumble. It seemed being questioned had gotten her all worked up.

What a troublesome girl… Since urging her had done nothing to help his situation, Zagan simply stared at Nephteros and waited for her to respond. Eventually, she seemed to realize he was waiting for her to act. And then, she stuck out what she was carrying in her arms, a conflicted look on her face.

"Here, I came to return your mantle."

"My mantle?" Zagan remembered what she was talking about as the words left his mouth.

Now that I think about it, I gave this to her when she lost her clothes on the boat, didn't I? Zagan had saved Nephteros when she was transformed into a monster by the residual thoughts of the Demon Lord. And at that time, he lent her the mantle in question.

"That's odd. You came all the way here just to return it?"

"Weren't you the one who said I had to return it myself!?"

"I did?" Zagan was focused on brewing up his 'gift' to Bifrons back then, so he didn't really remember much of what he said. At any rate, she brought it over all the way to him. He had to accept it graciously.

"Hm? Was it always this... pretty?" Nephy had mended it a number of times, but the fabric was quite old. Moreover, he remembered it being damaged heavily during his battle with the Sludge Demon Lord. And, as Zagan tilted his head to the side in confusion, Nephteros averted her gaze from him. The tips of her ears had started to go red.

"Fixing up tattered clothing is the least I can do."

"You mended it for me? Good job," Zagan said as he tried on the mantle, a strained smile on his face.

"Wow, not bad. If you ever get fed up with Bifrons, come to my castle. There's a whole mountain of work waiting for you."

"...Do you take me for some sort of laundry lady?"

"No, you also happen to know a lot about celestial mysticism, so you're far more than that."

"Well, I'll think about it," Nephteros replied, scoffing back at him as if she didn't hate the idea entirely. At the very least, Zagan couldn't sense any enthusiasm or disdain in her words.

"I assume things are going well with Bifrons?"

"I wonder..." Nephteros pulled a piece of paper out from the mantle as she said that. On first glance, it appeared to be the invitation Bifrons sent Zagan, but there was a unique mechanism woven into it. One that made a mana-powered fist swoop down on Bifrons any time they angered Nephteros.

"Oh, yeah. Allow me to thank you for this little trinket. It's taught Master Bifrons the importance of personal space."

"Now that's unexpected. You sure he learned his lesson? Doesn't really seem like the learning type..."

"Master Bifrons' head has been blown off several times already. It's like they say: fear is a powerful motivator," Nephteros claimed as she shook her head in exasperation.

"Hmmm…" Zagan hadn't expected that response.

Bifrons still can't defend against it? Bifrons was an Archdemon. Sure, Zagan set up a fairly intricate trap, but someone so powerful should have overcome it already. Plus, he could have just confiscated the letter if it really came down to it. The fact that Bifrons hadn't done so already meant they wanted it in place. Perhaps Bifrons actually had learned 'the importance of personal space,' as Nephteros put it.

…Though, it was also possible Bifrons had a weird fetish.

"Well, that's fortunate, isn't it? Next time, I'll take measures to keep you from being used as a guinea pig," Zagan said, a fleeting smile gracing his face.

Nephteros stiffened up and stared at the sight in wonder. Then, she turned bright red and hid her face in embarrassment.

"Th-That's none of your business. Really, I'm surprised you're so ki… I mean, I'm surprised you're so hospitable. I'm the one who tried to hurt Nephy, remember?"

"Nephy and I don't have time to dwell on a brat throwing a temper tantrum," Zagan said, looking about ready to burst into laughter.

"A brat? Look, I'm not sure how old you are, but I'm older than Nephelia, got it?"

"I see," Zagan muttered with a nod, then continued, "Now that I think of it, how old are you?" Zagan knew it was rude to ask a lady for her age, but he wasn't one to be bound by societal norms.

"I-I'm…. Huh? I… am…?" Nephteros was left daunted by his rather blunt question. She began cradling her head, clearly confused and unable to pin down an answer.

"What's wrong?"

"No… It's… nothing," Nephteros claimed before glaring back at Zagan.

"More importantly, even if you are an Archdemon, you should know it's rude to ask a lady for her age."

"You're the one who brought up the subject. I don't have any interest in your age..." Zagan said as he raised both his hands to surrender.

"Hmph..." Nephteros' silver hair swayed as she scoffed at him and walked down the corridor.

"It can't be... Does she not know her age?" Zagan muttered to himself gravely. That was a bad sign.

Zagan was left frozen in place, fearing the worst, for a quite a while after that exchange.

"...I can't sleep," Nephy mumbled in a puzzled tone for the millionth time that night. She had gotten her own room but was unable to sleep due to all the thoughts running through her mind.

"...Master Zagan," Nephy desperately called out to him. However, this was not his castle. He had his own bed for once, so he was probably fast asleep.

Is sleeping in the same bed as him out of the question? Would that bother him? He had allowed her to sit on his lap many times by that point, but they had only slept in each other's arms twice. There was the evening Zagan purchased Nephy, and the night Zagan revealed his past to her.

From time to time, Nephy found that her bed got cold. And whenever that happened, she prayed to sleep under the same covers as him in order to press into his warm, comforting body. Unfortunately, Zagan always slept atop his throne, which kept them apart.

I'm acting far too spoiled... Nephy shook her head in a fluster as her thoughts began to run wild. She was rather worried about what Zagan would think of her if she acted on her desires. She chose to believe he felt the exact same way, but that didn't mean he would reciprocate.

Of course, no matter what she did, Zagan would accept her. She knew that. However, it was still difficult to put herself out there.

Nephy's ears turned completely red as she began writhing around in her bed. She could hardly contain her imagination.

"I really can't sleep..." Nephy gave up after twisting and turning a few more times and got up off her bed. After stretching her hand out to the bedside table, she snapped her thin fingers, lighting the candle on it. That was basic sorcery Zagan taught her.

Next, Nephy tried opening the window. Though it was a window, it was made of simple wood planks, and there wasn't anything like glass set in it. By using the pole attached to each plank, you could pull them to the side to open them.

Moonlight streamed into the room as Nephy stared fixedly at one of the houses in the ruined village. That one just happened to be the place she was raised.

"...Odd. I don't particularly feel anything," Nephy said as she held her hand to her chest. Her pulse was the same as always, her breathing was normal, and she didn't feel the least bit nervous.

I thought it would hurt more... Even Zagan seemed fairly worried about her, which was why he tagged along. And yet, she was so calm that her return was anti-climactic. If elven corpses were strewn about, she may have at least felt pain in her heart, but there weren't even any traces of blood, and the buildings were largely intact. It was as if the residents had just vanished.

The tranquility of it all made her doubt that she actually lived there only a few months ago. No, that was a little wrong. It felt more like she'd returned to how she used to be before she met Zagan.

"Oh, I see. I used to feel like this all the time."

She was raised in an environment where great expectations resulted in great pain. Nobody would even look at her, and her mere presence was considered an evil influence.

That was why Nephy shut herself off from the world. If she stopped thinking, the pain eased a little. If she stopped moving, the pain became easier to handle. In exchange for not feeling pain, she was no longer able to feel joy. And so, all she did was sit still and pray her meaningless life would come to a swift end.

Her heart came to a standstill. She became an empty husk once more. However, that was no good. She had to come to terms with her past. Otherwise, traveling back to her hometown was pointless. If she continued to give in to her horrid memories, she would never again feel the warmth of love from Zagan and the rest of her family.

"I don't want that…" Nephy no longer wanted to die. In fact, it was no exaggeration to say her life only began the moment she met Zagan. She wanted to live for his sake. She wanted to continue her life with Zagan, Foll, Chastille, Manuela, Raphael, Gremory, Kimaris, and even Barbatos. That was why she simply had to cast aside her past self.

And, as she continued to stare at the house she once lived in to affirm her resolve…

"Huh…?" Nephy spotted a faint light in her old house.

Is somebody… still there? The windows were the same as the one Nephy was looking through, so a small amount of light seeped through the gaps in the wood planks. Something was up.

For all she knew, it could have been a traveler or a bandit, but it definitely wasn't a natural occurrence.

"I must notify Master Zagan immediately..." Nephy started heading toward Zagan's room when her feet suddenly came to a stop.

Is that really alright, I wonder...? Did Zagan really need to know? If he listened to her and investigated her old house, wouldn't he just do all the work as she sat back and relaxed? How exactly was she overcoming her old, weak self if she just let him protect her over and over?

"...My apologies, Master Zagan. Forgive me for acting of my own volition," Nephy said as she shook her head.

And at that moment, for the very first time, Nephy walked forward on her own two feet with no one there to support her.

Nephy slipped on her boots, then took a pen in hand and began scribbling down what had happened and what she was about to do. She was dead set on following through with her plan, but she was unsure how it would turn out in the end. Disappearing without a word would have been in poor taste, so she finished writing a memo before she jumped out the window.

It's really cold... Nephy was wearing her usual maid outfit near snowcapped mountains, which obviously left her trembling.

"Half a year ago, I wouldn't even have been able to feel the cold..."

Did that just mean she had gotten weaker? *Well, I can accept that sort of weakness.*

Honestly, she wanted Zagan to develop the same type of weaknesses that she had. That man was far too strong. He had

learned to rely on others somewhat recently, but there were still parts of him that wished to take care of everything on his own. And Nephy believed that being able to do everything resulted in more worries. She wished that he was weaker so he'd be forced to accept help from all sorts of people. Otherwise, everyone's gratitude would never get through to him.

"I want to grow strong enough to have Master Zagan rely on me..." Nephy muttered as she was taking the first steps toward achieving that goal. After crossing over the open space, she rushed to her old home. Though, it was never exactly home to her. In fact, she could only stay in one corner of the storehouse. The only time she was ever allowed into other rooms was to help out with cleaning or other chores.

She knew absolutely nothing about the other residents. Forget family, the people she'd lived with for the first sixteen years of her life weren't even her acquaintances.

Nephy's hand began trembling slightly as she moved to open the door, but this time, it wasn't due to the cold. She was scared. However, oddly enough, she was relieved by the sight.

It's alright. I'm not the same person anymore... Her emotions were functioning properly, which meant she was ready to face whatever was beyond that door. Clutching her chest with her left hand, Nephy took a deep breath and twisted the doorknob.

"...Huh?"

Warm air rushed out from the other side of the door. Upon taking a closer look, Nephy noticed the fireplace was lit. It seemed that was the source of light she spotted from her room.

Wish me luck, Master Zagan... Nephy thought as she stared back at the elder's manor.

She knew Zagan would be furious when he found out, but this was a problem Nephy had to face on her own. And so, Nephy took a step into the house she once lived in.

The place looked largely the same as the elder's manor. The floor was made of wood planks, but the walls were just moss-covered stones piled atop each other. Surprisingly, despite the simplistic windows, there wasn't even so much as a draft. The room was quite warm, which probably served to push the cold air back, but Nephy knew that would quickly change if the fireplace was extinguished.

The interior of the room hadn't changed at all. There were several paintings hung on each wall, and a small altar was installed near the entryway that they used to offer prayers to at mealtime. Other than that, there was a single dilapidated table with four wooden chairs around it. Seemed like the place belonged to a family of four.

She hadn't walked around the house enough to be familiar with it, but nothing looked out of place. In fact, it looked exactly the same as when the humans attacked the village, which had Nephy questioning her memory.

The people of this house are likely all dead... Nephy found that unfortunate, even though she knew those people cursed her with their dying breath. She may not have known them enough to mourn them, but she did pity them.

After mulling over her thoughts for a while, Nephy surveyed the rest of the house. And despite the fact that the fireplace was lit, there wasn't even any trace of footprints to be found.

She was looking around restlessly, doing her best to find a lead, when one of the paintings on the wall suddenly caught her attention. There was only a single artist in the entire village, and he always gifted families a painting to go along with each new baby. That was

why there should have been as many paintings as children in this house, but…

"My painting… isn't here?" Nephy never had a chance to take a close look at the place before, so that fact had escaped her. Perhaps they didn't want to hang up a painting of a cursed child, or maybe the artist himself refused to make one. However…

"Where exactly was I born?"

This had to be her hometown, but she had failed to find any definitive proof that she was born and raised here. Thus far, she had believed the people of this house were her blood relatives, but was that really the case? Would her own family have hated her for no reason?

What am I thinking? Parental bonds are a myth… Even Zagan was left alone in the world, forced to fend for himself from a young age. Forget his parents' faces, he didn't even know their names. If they were somehow still alive, they would have no connection to speak of.

Surely, such fickle bonds were naught but illusion. Or at least, that was what Nephy believed.

Being with all these people who aren't related to me by blood… is far better.

Zagan, who was a complete stranger, was the first one to truly ever make Nephy feel loved. And the first ones to call her a friend were Chastille and Manuela, who she had only just met recently. After that, Foll came along as a daughter of sorts, which made her feel like part of a family for the very first time.

Not a single one of them were related to her by blood. There were no such bonds tying them at all together, and that was no issue.

I must… figure out who I really am…. And just as she thought that, the painting that she was gazing at began to distort.

87

"Huh…?" Nephy watched on as four shadows slipped out of the painting in front of her. She could immediately tell they were the figures of the family who lived here.

An illusion? Nephy cast her gaze around her surroundings, but was unable to find the origin. Zagan probably would have been able to identify the location of the sorcerer at a glance, but Nephy was nowhere near as skilled as him. When it came to just sorcery, even the sorcerers working at the castle all surpassed her. Having said that, mysticism wasn't a power that always manifested the desired result, which made it a completely unknown element. There was no guarantee she was their better even with it added into the mix.

Each of the illusions took a seat around the table, then began cheerfully laughing. They were the spitting image of a happy family.

I've never seen that look on their faces… Nephy had only ever had scorn or disgust directed at her. She couldn't possibly have imagined them laughing merrily.

"They look so happy…" Nephy muttered. And then, that happy scene began melting away in response. The next illusion was one filled with dead bodies. Their once-smiling faces were tainted by the bright red blood flowing from their heads, and their mouths were belting out words of pain and resentment.

'Why didn't you save us?' they asked. 'I don't want to die,' they wailed. 'Nephy should have died instead,' they complained.

"You have the right to resent me…" Nephy knew that she may have been able to save them if she had fought against the invading humans. But instead, she had allowed them to be slaughtered, and that was something she would regret for the rest of her life.

Witnessing the agony that they went through pained Nephy. Surely, if they had met under different circumstances, they could

have gotten along. Or perhaps, as she was now, she could have developed an actual relationship with them.

"However…" Nephy mumbled as the image of the corpses was burned into her mind, then continued, "If it was that painful, why didn't you protect each other?"

I would put my life on the line to protect Zagan or Foll, so shouldn't these people have done the same? Nephy would never have been willing to just cower and die like these elves. And as she spurned their memories with such thoughts, the illusion of the corpses shattered like glass, and darkness enveloped her once more. Except this time, even the light from the fireplace had vanished.

It's cold… The once warm room had chilled immensely. The sudden change even had Nephy wondering if the fireplace had actually been lit at all. She looked over to it, but couldn't sense any heat coming off it. Even if a fire were extinguished with water, the heat from the firewood should still have remained. And at that moment, everything clicked into place.

Was I… lured out here…? In the end, it may have been better to at least alert Zagan before coming here. However, Nephy did not regret her decision.

The culprit should be around here somewhere… Nephy braced herself as she took another look around the place, but she was only met by a mocking laugh.

"Kufufu, how brave…"

Nephy was horrified by that voice, which was accompanied by a shadow stretching out of the floor. On top of the room being dimly lit, the shadow was wearing a hood, so she couldn't tell if it was a man or woman. However, based on their voice, she did know it was someone considerably older.

This person is far stronger than me...! Nephy raised her guard as she shifted her focus over to the exit. She had learned the basics of sorcery and could use mysticism quite freely in this specific location, which meant celestial mysticism wasn't out of the question. If she fought without worrying about her own safety, she could defeat even a skilled sorcerer. Unfortunately, she could tell the person before her was a step above that.

I must survive and return to Master Zagan's side... If she didn't, he would feel responsible for her death and blame himself for not being by her side. Nephy wanted to be Zagan's pillar of support, so she couldn't possibly make him suffer that.

That was why Nephy's number one priority was returning to his side. The true identity of the shadow, as well as why it lured her out alone, was irrelevant in the face of that desire.

Sadly, I have to stand and fight... There would have been no point in her heading out alone if she tried to run away just because her opponent was stronger than her.

She had to fight, survive, and return alive. That was the result Nephy desired. And having come to that conclusion, she opened her mouth to speak.

"Why... did you show me that?"

"Hmm... You're not running away or anything, huh?" the shadow unexpectedly replied. After that, she could somehow tell its mouth warped into a smile before saying, "So, how was it? The figure of those who tormented you being punished, I mean."

"...It was the worst possible feeling," Nephy replied. It had felt like she killed the same people twice.

This is not a place for me to bend a knee and yield... Nephy was only permitted to collapse in the presence of Zagan. And since she

came here without his permission, she was not allowed to break down and cry.

The shadow then stuck out a hand that resembled a dead branch and touched its own jaw with it.

"How interesting. You're surprisingly straightforward for someone who's been forced to lock away her emotions her whole life. I can also sense a strong will to live within you... You should have obtained a fragment of celestial mysticism, right? And yet, you're not the least bit arrogant... Very interesting indeed."

They've seen through everything... Nephy thought as she bit down on her lip. It seemed this shadow knew everything about her. Bifrons was clearly not the only one who was monitoring her and Zagan.

"Hm... You truly mourn the death of such riff-raff? Amazing. You believe in second chances for even the most heinous villains... and grieve over the loss of such possibilities. How noble."

Nephy was taken aback by the ideas the shadow was expressing, which seemed almost ripped straight from her mind.

"Just... what are you?" Nephy forced that question out as she trembled in fear. However, the shadow simply replied in a carefree tone.

"Oh dear, my apologies. At my age, I don't get the chance to meet new people often."

The shadow removed their hood as they said that, revealing an old woman with white hair. She possessed a stern gaze that exceeded anything Gremory had ever shot at Nephy, which was accentuated by her all-too-familiar azure eyes.

It can't be... Is she...? Nephy gulped as she took in those eyes and ears that seemed so similar to hers.

"I am the one who carries the fate of this village, the..."

Nephy cut her off and took action. This old woman was too dangerous. Bifrons was amicable compared to her.

Spirits of the forest, answer my call! The roots of the trees around the village reached far under the ground, so Nephy's call reached them even though she was inside a building.

Roots shot through the floorboards one after the other due to Nephy's mysticism. The only attack she could use with sorcery was a blade of flame, and celestial mysticism required her to sing, so that was her only option. Unfortunately, the roots failed to capture anything.

"She's gone…?"

The old woman shook and vanished from sight.

That wasn't her real body? Even now, the land obeyed Nephy's will, but it couldn't find any trace of her.

Does that mean the threat is gone? Nephy's opponent had power that far outstripped hers, but she had left her alone.

"Have I become a stronger person now?"

It sure didn't feel like it. Nephy had stood up to the old woman, but it seemed like she didn't even spare her a second thought. Dumbfounded by the situation, she just stood around for a while before returning to her senses.

"That's right. I have to report this to Master Zagan…" Nephy felt that Zagan needed to know about this mysterious old woman. And so, she turned toward the front door, but found herself interrupted by ominous laughter. It was a deep, gloomy, and creepy cackle that echoed through Nephy's head and distorted her vision. However, there wasn't anyone around who could be the source, which left her perplexed.

Did she set this up before she left…? Nephy was capable of crushing the entire house and dragging it underground, but she

wasn't sure that would do anything. Moreover, there was a possibility that the thing Zagan was looking for was here in this house, so she couldn't take that risk.

Still, Nephy couldn't think of any other options. And so, she slowly walked out of the house with her guard up. For whatever reason, the laughing stopped as soon as she stepped outside.

What's happening? She had felt quite dizzy at first, but now she was fine. Pleasantly surprised by the turn of events, she started walking toward the elder's manor, but...

"H-Huh?" Nephy's feet buckled, leaving her unable to walk properly. *Wait, am I even standing up right now? It looks a lot like I'm crawling instead... My body won't move the way I want it to...*

The night grew colder, but even so, Nephy somehow managed to struggle over to the elder's manor.

"Mashter... Zagan..." Nephy was speaking with a lisp, presumably because of the cold weather, as she stretched out her hand out to the doorknob. However, she found herself unable reach it. Upon closer inspection, she noticed that her hands were completely hidden inside her sleeve, and her boots were suddenly oversized.

Something's wrong with my body... Nephy didn't understand what was going on, which made her knock on Zagan's door sound all the more desperate.

"Mashter Zagan..."

Surprisingly, the door slammed open before even a second passed.

"Nephy!" Zagan roared. He stretched out his arms to embrace her, but immediately stiffened, a shocked expression on his face.

"Are you really Nephy? What's with that body?"

"Huh...?" Nephy looked down at her body again, at which point she realized that her clothes were far too big for her. Confused, she

93

tried touching her own face, which was oddly squishy and stretchy. And as a final test, she moved her tongue around the inside of her mouth, which made it clear that not all her teeth had popped out yet. After confirming all that, the truth finally dawned on her.

Nephy had turned into a small child.

Chapter III ✡ An Archdemon's Dilemma: How to Love An Elf Child

"Wow, she came back as a kid, huh?" Barbatos said as he tried to poke Little Nephy's cheeks.

It was still late at night. Zagan had immediately rushed outside when he realized Nephy was missing, but he found her on the other side of the door, seemingly de-aged. Unsure how to deal with the situation, Zagan gathered everyone in the living room. He had managed to get Foll, Chastille, Nephteros, and Barbatos.

Gremory and Kimaris weren't there. The two of them went to investigate the house Nephy had visited. This was because sorcery that manipulated age was Gremory's field of expertise, and Kimaris could track people by scent. They left the window open so that the two of them could report back the moment they found anything.

Zagan looked down at his lap... where the now tiny Nephy was sound asleep. Her usual maid outfit was too baggy to wear, so she'd changed into some children's clothing that they'd found in the manor. It was quite old, yet still cute, with frilly lace decorating the collar and skirt. It looked more like formal wear than anything, but beggars couldn't be choosers.

Foll was gently brushing Nephy's head. Judging from her appearance, she looked to be about five or six years old. It was difficult to judge the age of a child, but it was certain that she was under ten, which left her looking younger than Foll.

Nephy tried her best to explain the situation, but walking through the cold had left her winded. She ended up dozing off before they got any relevant information. Luckily, she had left a clue beforehand...

"This note was left behind in Nephy's room. It reads, 'I saw a light in my house, so I'm going to investigate it.'"

"Why the hell'd she go off on her own? Doesn't she always ask for Zagan's opinion before doing something?" Barbatos inquired, a puzzled expression on his face. Even Barbatos, of all people, seemed to understand Nephy fairly well. Next, Chastille took the note from Barbatos' hand.

"You really don't get it, do you? It was her old house, a place full of awful memories. Do you really not understand the sense of shame and embarrassment she must have felt?" Chastille asked as she ripped the note out of Barbatos' hands.

"No way in hell I'd understand crap like that."

Chastille glared at Barbatos in response, but it didn't have much effect.

This is all my fault. I should have kept her by my side at all times... Sure, Zagan knew Nephy must have thought things through before taking action, but that didn't make him feel any better. He wanted to commend her determination, but he wished they could have just talked things through and worked together from the start. Then, things wouldn't have turned out so bad.

"Zagan, can you turn Nephy back?" Foll asked.

"I'll show you that I can," Zagan immediately replied. However, he wasn't actually so sure. And it seemed he'd done a poor job of hiding that unease, as Barbatos raised an eyebrow.

"Hold up. If you could fix things, she'd be back to normal already... You can't break down this sorcery, can you?"

"…It's not sorcery."

"Say what?"

That was the reason Zagan was making such a grim expression.

"Nephy wasn't turned into a child by sorcery. It's mysticism, or if not that, something even more ancient, like a dragon or god's curse."

In other words, it was something even Sorcerer Slayer Zagan could not overcome.

"It's… not a dragon's curse. It's something else. Maybe something even more powerful…" Foll claimed as she placed her hand on the sleeping Nephy's forehead. She may have been young, but Foll was still a dragon, so she was most likely correct.

"…I think it's mysticism," Nephteros declared.

"Are you certain?"

"I can't say for sure, but it feels quite similar… Still, that's odd. The only living high elves in the world, let alone this village, are Nephelia and I."

"Think you can break it?"

"That would be quite difficult. Master Bifrons never taught me anything like this. Maybe you can ask them for help, but…" Nephteros was being rather vague, but her expression relayed that she thought it best not to consult Bifrons.

Suits me just fine. Don't really want to end up indebted to that guy… Even if they did go to Bifrons, there was no trusting that shady Archdemon. Bifrons would probably just abduct Nephy under the pretense of examination.

"It'll take some time, but I'll try looking into it… I hate to say this, but that old… Gremory is probably your best bet," Nephteros proclaimed as she begrudgingly gave credit to the woman who had harassed her earlier.

It was certainly true that Gremory could change her age with sorcery, which did make her their most valuable asset on this case. Nephteros' response was sound, which surprised Zagan and made him turn a warm gaze over to her.

"Hm? What do you want?"

"Mmm... I just never expected you to actually want to help Nephy."

"D-Don't misunderstand! I'm indebted to you, so this is just my way of paying you back! Besides, I can't exactly leave after putting you in a bad mood earlier, right?" Nephteros said, her ears turning bright red as she continued to ramble.

"Man, you're a pretty annoying girl..." Barbatos muttered in an exasperated tone.

"...What are you trying to say?" Nephteros inquired as she glared back at him, but Barbatos simply shrugged his shoulders in response.

"I understand you completely!" Chastille claimed as she clasped Nephteros' shoulder with a burning gaze. She seemed to think she'd found a kindred spirit.

"About how I find this man irritating and want to kill him?"

"That too, but I'm talking about how you're a truly kind person at heart!"

"Wha... Wh-Wh-What?!" Nephteros' ears were dyed bright red as they began flapping about. It seemed that she was completely thrown out of sorts, since she wasn't even able to coldly retort as she usually did.

"Oh, come on, why do you guys hate me so much? I've saved your skin a ton of times, remember...?" Barbatos was muttering something, seemingly depressed, but that didn't really matter.

I see. If Nephteros slips up even a little, she ends up the same as Chastille, huh? Sure, she wasn't breaking down like a crybaby, but the way she looked when Gremory was toying around with her reminded Zagan of Chastille's tear-stained face.

The person in question seemed self-conscious of that fact, since she shrank back with a pale face, then shook her head in a fluster.

"I don't enjoy being bullied like you do!"

"…Isn't that a little rude?" Chastille looked downright depressed. It seemed being rejected by a potential comrade was far too much for her to bear.

At that exact moment, Gremory and Kimaris returned from Nephy's house.

"We've returned, my Archdemon," Gremory said.

"…How was it?" Zagan asked. Unfortunately, the two of them shook their heads.

"There are traces of something being used, but the caster is long gone."

"Their scent was also erased, so I was unable to track them. I'm sorry."

They were facing an opponent who could turn Nephy into a child before she even knew it, so he wasn't surprised that they covered all their tracks.

"Good work. There's something I'd like your help with starting tomorrow, so get some rest," Zagan offered his thanks to the pair as he let out a sigh.

"Hm…" Gremory nodded at his words as she adjusted the scythe on her shoulder, but it was clear to Zagan that something was wrong.

"Is something bothering you, Gremory?"

"...Only a little. It's just, the traces of power I saw seemed awfully familiar."

"Really?"

"It's just a hunch. I don't actually know its true nature, but..." Gremory trailed off before shaking her head and saying, "Well, I'll report back to you right away if I remember anything. Don't get your hopes too high, though."

"No, I'm relying on you," Zagan said, asserting his belief. Even if they were unable to break the curse itself, Gremory's sorcery had the potential to help cure Nephy.

Both Gremory and Kimaris were taken aback by Zagan's reply, so they simply stared back at him in wonder for a while before responding.

"Keeheehee, you're quite the sweet talker, aren't you? Well, if my Archdemon is relying on me, I can't afford to cut any corners."

"I shall also do everything in my power to aid you," Kimaris proclaimed.

"You're relying on them...?" Nephteros watched the two of them intently as she said that. Her voice almost sounded envious. And honestly, Zagan could understand that feeling. After all, he had only learned the joy of relying on others and being relied on in return quite recently. Thankfully, that lesson had also made him realize he had to show others his sincerity, which was why Zagan repeated the same words to Nephteros.

"I'm also relying on you, Nephteros. You're the only one of us who knows a thing about mysticism."

"...I-I already agreed to cooperate, didn't I?" Nephteros turned her face away as she said that, but Zagan could tell her ears were quivering happily.

101

I'm not sure who's stupid enough to mess with Nephy, but I'll be sure to make them regret it.

In general, anger was a prime motivator, and Zagan was positively seething. He had trouble containing the burning rage that was coursing through his veins, and he eagerly awaited the chance to direct it straight into the source of all his frustrations.

However, unfortunately for Zagan, things didn't go according to his plan at all.

"Mashter Zagan! What's this?" Nephy asked as she dug up a frog who was in the middle of hibernating in the forest.

"That creature… is known as a frog. It's edible, so we can at least use it as an emergency ration."

"I-I could never!"

"Only if you're ever starving. It looks like it's still hibernating, so put it back where you found it for now."

"Hibernating…?"

"This sort of creature can't gather much food in the winter, which makes it resort to sleeping through most of it."

"Mashter Zagan's amazing! You know everything, don't you!?"

"…Not really."

The next morning, Nephy's mind had regressed to match her outer appearance. By the time morning rolled around, she had completely forgotten what happened the previous night. Having said that, it wasn't like she forgot about Zagan and the others. In fact, she was actually quite attached to them.

"Nephy, let's go bury it," Foll said from right beside Nephy.

"Yes, Big Shish!" Nephy responded as she tottered along behind Foll. It seemed that Nephy's change had resulted in them getting closer. Foll also seemed to quite like being called a big sister, and she continued to lead Nephy by the hand all over the place.

Zagan was reading a book in the shade of a tree while watching over the two of them. Contrary to the graveness of the situation, the scene playing out before him was akin to a family picnic.

For the time being, I guess it's a good thing that Nephy isn't all that depressed... Luckily, she hadn't forgotten about Zagan and the others, or that might not have been true.

Zagan glanced behind him. Now that it was bright out, the others had begun investigating the village. None of them knew exactly what happened to Nephy's body, so Zagan and Foll ended up staying by her side.

Barbatos, who had deep shadows beneath his eyes and whose speech and conduct were damaged beyond repair. Gremory, who had once more returned to the form of an old woman and was far too untrustworthy. Kimaris, who had the face of a lion that could kill a beast with a single glare. Nephteros, who upon their first meeting, only ever scowled at people. And Zagan, who, needless to say, did not have a countenance that attracted children at all. At best, the only person around who a child would trust upon a first meeting was the crybaby, Chastille. No child would survive in such a hostile environment.

Zagan looked over to see how his companions were doing. Perhaps having noticed that, Chastille walked over to him with a bored expression on her face.

"How's it going here, Zagan?"

"Foll's doing great with Nephy. Unfortunately, I haven't been able to find anything of particular use."

Of course, it wasn't like Zagan was just babysitting. Next to him was a pile of journals that he found in the manor. They were the journals of the village elders that spanned generations.

"Can you read elven writing?" Chastille muttered in admiration.

"Celestian is another matter, but I can understand their common tongue to an extent, yes," Zagan said. Then, he threw a question back at Chastille, "Is everything fine on your end?"

"Sorry, but my knowledge of elves and sorcery can't compare to any of you. I'll probably be more useful as Nephy's bodyguard…" Chastille replied in a dignified manner that made her usual crybaby persona seem utterly fake. And after that, she cast her gaze downward and said, "Do you think there are any clues in those elven journals?"

"Well, right now I'm looking for records of those who left the village or descriptions of heretics who idolized sorcery. They can't be all that common in an elven village. And since they went out of their way to make a move on us out here, it's only natural to believe that they have some connection to this place."

Based on what Nephteros and Gremory had said, the culprit was definitely an elf.

"I get that much, but how will finding a description of them help?" Chastille asked, a confused expression on her face.

"Most elves can't survive out in the world. If they left the village, they would need to create some sort of barrier with sorcery. And in that case, I can track the sorcery as long as I find out what it is."

Elves were hunted by regular people and sorcerers alike. Nephy being auctioned off was one such example. The only way for them to protect themselves was to master sorcery and make use of their massive reservoirs of mana. And if they were using sorcery, Archdemon Zagan would definitely be able to corner them.

In other words, the documents he was pouring over were his best leads. However...

"Why the long face?"

"Hmm..." Zagan let out a puzzled groan as he flipped through the pages of one of the books.

"None of these mention Nephy at all."

"Are they not just journals from before Nephy was born?" Chastille asked as she stared back at him in wonder.

"They aren't. The journals end with a description of how humans invaded their territory. I assume they scribbled it down right before the village was destroyed. And I know for a fact that Nephy was there when that happened."

"I heard Nephy was, um, called a cursed child here, right? Then, isn't it safe to conclude that she was being ignored?" Chastille muttered, deep in thought.

"If I was in their shoes, I would have kept a constant eye on such a dangerous brat. The fact that they didn't makes it clear that they understood Nephy's power. I mean, they even begged her for help in the end, didn't they?"

"You're right... If they actually thought she was dangerous, then they would have paid more attention to her..." Chastille muttered as she gathered her thoughts. Then, a look of enlightenment graced her face, and she said, "Wait, wouldn't there be a journal dedicated entirely to Nephy's surveillance? I'm sure the elves hated her, but acting up in public was probably frowned upon, right? Isn't it possible that they hid any information on her from the other villagers?"

Zagan's mouth popped open in surprise. He never expected to hear such wise words coming from her.

"Huh? What's wrong?"

"No, it's just... I'm surprised that you had such a good idea."

"What do you take me for!?" Chastille exclaimed as her face spasmed in shock and anger.

"Try saying that after you stop being a crybaby."

"I just try to keep my public and private faces separate, that's all. And I've judged the current situation to be a part of my public duty."

In other words, despite being a fairly capable Angelic Knight, this girl's a complete wreck in her private life? Zagan was left at his wit's end by her response. Thinking back on it, she actually seemed quite dignified and prudent when they fought for the first time. At that time, she had challenged Zagan due to her mission as an Angelic Knight. And then, when Nephy reunited with her in town, she was a total crybaby. That was when she was relieved of her duties as an Angelic Knight, which made sense thanks to all the new information she just provided. After that, she only ever met Zagan when she was off duty, cementing her status as a complete crybaby.

Chastille's ability to so clearly split the two parts of her was worthy of praise, but that made one wonder why she couldn't at least retain some of her composure in private. Not that it mattered in the end, though. In fact, her split personalities proved quite useful in this case.

"I have a request. Bring over every single elven book you can find in the elder's manor. Just look for anything written in Elvish and bring it over!" Zagan looked up from his book as he asked her for that favor.

"So you're saying it might be hidden in plain sight, huh?"

"Exactly. How clever, Chastille."

"U-Uh, thanks... Ehehe..." Chastille's face slackened for a moment, but then she immediately regained her composure and ran over to the elder's manor.

I can't believe she's acting like this and being a big help... Something's wrong with this village.

Completely unfamiliar and abnormal phenomenon were occurring left and right. However, if Chastille was willingly casting aside her crybaby persona and taking this seriously, there was no way Zagan could just play around. And so, he continued to scan through the pile of journals at his side.

Unfortunately, he failed to find Nephy's name anywhere, even after he went through fifty years' worth of journals. And while he sat there, puzzled by that turn of events, he felt something weigh down on his head.

"Ehehe..."

Zagan looked up and caught sight of a tiny Nephy with an enormous smile on her face.

Why are you so damn cute?! Nephy's smile brightened his once gloomy heart. Zagan could barely contain himself anymore. The urge to protect her was overflowing from within him. And because of that, his body ignored his mind and he ended up giving her a ride on his shoulders.

"Wooow, I'm up sooo high!"

"Zagan, me too!" Foll exclaimed.

"Gaaah, fine!" Zagan said as he moved Nephy over to his left shoulder in order to make room on his right for Foll. And then, he ran a lap around the plaza with the two of them up there.

Kimaris, who was investigating the other houses in the village, seemed to want to join them, but he ended up controlling himself.

"That was fun."

"It was! Big Shish!"

Foll let out a sigh of satisfaction, and Nephy was bouncing around next to her. After a moment of silence, Nephy began speaking with a smile plastered on her face.

"Mashter Zagan, I made a flower crown with Big Shish Foll! It's for you!"

"Y-Yeah, thanks…" Zagan replied in a bewildered tone. This was the first gift he'd ever received from Nephy, which meant he had to protect it. And so, Zagan used sorcery to keep the flowers from withering. However, as he did that, the tiny Nephy looked up at him with a worried look on her face.

"Do you feel better now, Mashter Zagan?"

"Do I… not look well?"

"Yeah. You usually seem to be having fun, but you looked really sad earlier, Mashter Zagan."

That was obviously because it was difficult to remain happy when the girl he loved was suffering under some kind of curse.

"So, here's a good luck charm to cheer you up," Nephy said as she stretched out with her tiny arms to grab Zagan's cheeks. After getting a firm grip on them, she rubbed her forehead against his. The sensation was all too familiar. Or well, of course it was, since he'd done something similar in the past when he was trying to help Nephy.

This girl really is the same at heart, huh? Even after shrinking, losing her most recent memories, and having her personality reduced to that of an innocent child, Nephy was still Nephy. And that made Zagan extremely happy.

"What a useful charm. I see. I really do feel better now."

"Really? Ehehe…" Nephy said with a smile.

This Nephy really does smile a lot, doesn't she?

It was like she knew nothing of rejection or loss. She was the very definition of a pure little girl. Perhaps this was her true nature all along, and it went dormant due to the years of abuse she suffered in the village. He was happy that she had regained her smile, but the fact it only came back because she was turned into a child left Zagan feeling rather bitter.

In an attempt to banish such thoughts, Zagan tried touching the flower crown Nephy made for him. When he did, he noticed that it was made of beautiful violet flowers.

"I'm surprised such delicate flowers bloom in this weather."

The seasons were beginning to transition toward winter even back in Kianoides, which meant Norden, a typically cold country, was already in full-blown winter. That was why Zagan was so surprised by any flowers being in bloom.

"Those are violets. They aren't in season right now," Foll said as she tilted her head to the side in confusion.

"…What do you mean?" Zagan asked in a tone that made it clear he was just as puzzled as Foll. In response, Foll just pointed up at the sky. And when he looked up, he saw… a swarm of butterflies fluttering about.

"…Huh?" Zagan stood up as a shocked expression rose to his face, then said, "Butterflies… in this cold weather?"

Butterflies were a race closely linked to fairies, which made their wings ideal catalysts for sorcery. That was why Zagan knew about them. Unlike most creatures, they could not survive through a harsh winter. If it was just a single one, then it was possible that it woke up by mistake, but a whole swarm was an entirely different

matter. After all, butterflies were so sensitive to the cold that they wouldn't even hatch unless they were in a warm climate.

Foll looked around the area, clearly confused. And as Zagan followed her gaze, he noticed something rather odd. The previous evening, the houses simply didn't have any people in them, and showed no signs of really wasting away. However, they were now overrun by ivy and moss. Additionally, flowers of every color bloomed on the ground, butterflies fluttered about looking for nectar, and a warm spring wind brushed against his cheeks. There was no way this made any sense. Such a huge shift couldn't have occurred in the time it took him to read through all those journals.

"The weather here has gone mad... No, the flow of time itself is weird. We should leave quickly..." Foll informed him of that fact in a voice filled with dread.

After taking notice of the irregularity, Zagan called everyone together. Nephteros, Barbatos, Kimaris, and Gremory were gathered. Searching about while in the form of an old woman seemed unbearable for her back, so she was currently in a more young, beautiful form.

Chastille, who was left in charge of searching the manor, had not returned. She had just began searching, which more than excused her absence, but Barbatos said that she found something of interest. For the time being, his shadow was connected to her, so it was fine even if they didn't forcibly call her back.

Nephy's high elf blood should have protected her against sorcery, but she was still turned into a child. I should've realized something stronger was at play... Zagan beat himself up about missing the

obvious. Somehow, he didn't even realize something was wrong until Foll pointed it out to him.

Zagan tried touching the ground. Even now, the earth was being pushed aside as new sprouts poked out their heads here and there. By evening, the area they were in would undoubtedly be completely covered in weeds. He could sense the flow of mana, and that told him this phenomenon was not 'something created' like when a person made use of sorcery. It was clearly unnatural, yet it was also natural in the same way the earth transformed over the course of months and years. It was like watching a sea of trees grow at an accelerated pace.

"So this is also mysticism? How troublesome. For the time being, should we get out of here?" said Zagan. He specialized in breaking sorcery, which meant he was totally out of his element. Plus, if the barrier around this land was responsible for turning Nephy into an infant, there was a chance that getting away from it would return her to normal. And honestly, even if that didn't work, it may have been best to have his subordinates seek refuge elsewhere.

"No, it's probably useless. Seems like the barrier is already covering the entire village. Someone like Purgatory may be able to slip through, though…" Gremory corrected the position of the large scythe on her shoulder and shook her head as she denied Zagan's suggestion.

"Is that true?" Zagan asked.

"Maybe if it's just me. Dragging a bunch of people through makes it pretty hard, though…" Barbatos replied, shrugging his shoulders all the while. The way he said that made it seem like he'd already tried and failed.

No dice, huh?

"My sense of smell has been limited. It's probable that we'll end up being transported right back even if we try to run away. Whoever is doing this is in total control..." Kimaris strained his face as he conveyed his thoughts.

"Even this Balor's Evil Eye of mine is sealed. It's probably the same for Valefor's breath..." Gremory possessed an evil eye that could turn anything she cast her gaze on to ash. It was an ability that some fomorians possessed which was different in nature from sorcery, and in some ways, it was even more powerful than mysticism.

"I see. We've basically been imprisoned inside this village, huh?"

Everyone fell silent as he voiced their collective thoughts on the matter. Nephy was the only one who didn't really understand, and she curiously tilted her head to the side.

"...What're we gonna do, Zagan?" Barbatos asked. However, instead of answering his question, Zagan simply put his hand on the ground and examined the flow of mana once more.

It's quite complex, but it's not like I can't read it, either... Based on his findings, there was likely a 'gap' somewhere. And Barbatos being able to escape at all supported his theory.

"By the way, Barbatos, do you remember what we had for breakfast?" Zagan questioned Barbatos in order to nail down specifics.

"Huh? The hell are you..." Barbatos raised his voice in anger, but went silent when he saw the serious expression on Zagan's face. Then, he thought it over and said, "Leftover soup and bread from yesterday, and salad made of wild plants, right? What about it?"

"Hm... Then Kimaris, can you talk about what's happened since Nephy ended up like this?"

"Sir Zagan, you told me and Miss Gremory to investigate Lady Nephy's old house because my nose is useful for tracking creatures, and Miss Gremory is well-versed in sorcery that manipulates age. And upon finding anything strange, we were to return without engaging in any hostilities…" Kimaris answered with a puzzled expression.

"Foll. Before coming here, you worked on a flower bed with Kimaris, right? What did you dig up back then?" Zagan finished things by questioning Foll.

"Huh…? A mandrake. It's tasty as a snack, and it also strengthens mana, so I was growing them with Kimry."

"That's right. Next time, let's try procuring some nice ones along with better soil."

"Mmm…" Foll purred and happily nodded at Kimaris' words as Zagan gently brushed his beloved daughter's head

"What's the point of all these questions?" Barbatos asked in a flustered tone.

"Let's see. For the time being, I can tell that all our memories are intact. Only Nephy is an exception…" Nephy's recent memories were all vague. If there was some sort of malevolent influence, it would likely have altered their memories of the last few days, as well. Zagan checked each of them just to be sure, but it seemed there was nothing out of the ordinary with any of their memories. Perhaps it was due to their race, as everyone in his group was different?

Regardless of the reason, they seemed fine mentally. Plus, he couldn't tell if their bodies were holding up okay. Though, sorcerers naturally resisted the effects of old age, so that wasn't actually much of a concern.

After confirming all those facts, Zagan explained his conclusion like it was no big deal.

"Well, we have ways of breaking through it by sheer force. For the time being, let's continue our investigation."

A time warp was certainly something to keep a cautious eye on, but there were no traces of any other threat. In that case, kicking up a fuss would accomplish nothing. That was the answer Zagan arrived at.

"Sheer force? This ain't a barrier made by sorcery, right? Is there something you can do?"

"Who cares if it isn't sorcery? We can still break through with sorcery, right?"

Sure, Zagan couldn't devour it, but that wasn't his only skill. He hadn't just been wasting his days away in his castle after he learned of celestial mysticism. In fact, he'd developed at least one means of dealing with such sticky situations.

This place will probably end up as scorched earth where not even a single blade of grass will grow, but it's not like anyone lives here anymore... The only doubt in his mind was if it was really alright to decimate Nephy's hometown. That was why he wanted to try and gather a few more clues. Also, Zagan came here to investigate the connection between celestial mysticism and Sacred Swords, so looking around more couldn't hurt.

"You know, putting it like that really stings. You make it sound like this isn't all that big a deal..." Gremory said, looking visibly depressed.

"That's just how it is. Leaving this place isn't all that hard. Plus, even if it was, I'd have you to help, so I was never worried."

In truth, this was an extremely powerful barrier that may have even transformed Nephy into an infant, which meant there was a chance that the same would eventually happen to Zagan and the

others. However, its power simply piqued Zagan's sense of curiosity. He wished to take his time and investigate its structure.

But I guess I'll have to end things early if they start getting nervous... Either way, this situation wasn't something they had to worry about. And, as Zagan's subordinates relaxed due to his lack of tension, Nephteros spoke up to challenge his resolve.

"Stop right there. I know what you may be thinking, but I can't do anything about this barrier. Celestial mysticism isn't all-powerful, so if you're planning to depend on me here..."

"I told you already, remember? You're a guest. A guest doesn't have to get riled up over such trivial matters!" Zagan bopped Nephteros on the head repeatedly as he said that.

"Huh...? What?" Nephteros made some sort of complicated happy-yet-embarrassed face, but she didn't brush away Zagan's hand.

"Big Shish Nephterosh is just like me..." Nephy said as she pulled on the hem of Nephteros' skirt.

"What? How?"

"You're happy that Mashter Zagan is patting your head!"

"N-No, that's not true!" Nephteros proclaimed, shaking off Nephy's hand.

"S-S-Sorry... I thought... you would be happy..." Nephy sobbed, seemingly shocked by Nephteros' actions.

"H-Hold on, this isn't something to cry over! I'm not mad or anything, I swear! Look, you can have Zagan pat your head to make you feel better, right?" Nephteros turned pale and panicked as tears appeared on Nephy's face. Then, she lifted Nephy into her arms and stuck her hand out toward Zagan in a plea for help.

"Hear me, Nephy. Nephteros doesn't hate you or anything. Even when she's happy, she's inclined to feel embarrassed if people point it out. You'd do well to sympathize with her condition."

"Really?"

"Y-Yeah, he's right…" Nephteros returned a reluctant nod when Nephy directed her innocent eyes at her.

"I really, really love Big Shish Nephterosh!" Nephy exclaimed, a bright and energetic smile on her face.

"Urgh… This… Uh… Er… Jeez…" Nephteros let out an exasperated sigh after waffling about for a while. The sight of her being unable to resist Little Nephy was cute. Especially considering the indifference she normally treated her with.

"Looks like you can't handle small children, huh?" Zagan teased her over that weakness. In response, she simply let out a snort with a 'hmph,' and lowered Nephy to the ground before speaking up.

"…That's not true. I just feel bad for them. Children are born free of any sin, right? Even you pretended to drop an apple to bless a waif on the roadside, didn't you?"

"…Hold on. How do you even know that?" Zagan's face stiffened upon hearing her mutter that so nonchalantly.

The other day, when Zagan traveled to Kianoides with Nephy, he spotted a homeless child squatting down on the corner of a street. And upon seeing that figure overlapping with that of his past, he blessed the child with an apple. Nephy had noticed, since she was right next to him, but she should've been the only witness.

Nephteros suddenly covered her mouth as if it were a slip of the tongue, but it was already too late. Forced to own up to her wrongdoings, she answered his question in a timid tone.

"Um… Master Bifrons prepared a crystal ball to monitor all of you, and I just so happened to see that happen when I took a quick peek…"

"That guy's still being a peeping Tom?"

117

"Th-That's right! I just happened to spot it by chance when Master Bifrons was peeping!"

Don't tell me Nephteros was peeping because she wanted to get along with Nephy? Zagan shot a look full of suspicion at her when he heard her flustered tone.

No matter how he looked at it, Zagan felt that this case didn't involve Bifrons at all. If Bifrons were involved, they wouldn't have just remained a spectator the entire time. Though, that left him wondering why Nephteros couldn't get along with Nephy when she was so concerned about her.

Still, I'd better stop now. I feel like this girl will act more stubborn if I keep teasing her... Perhaps that was the key difference between her and Chastille, who could put up with being teased for ages, but would rebound at the next moment's notice.

Chastille's ability to recover from insults was something else. She had a sturdiness to her that was akin to a weed. And because of that, people who teased her often forgot how to hold back and enjoyed themselves at her expense.

On the other hand, Nephteros didn't feel like as much of an easy target. Though, that made teasing her more fun. Still, Zagan was the one who labeled her his guest, so he knew he had to end things there.

"Well, I don't have any interest in what you lot are up to, so just tell Bifrons to keep the peeping in moderation. Next time, I won't let it go that easily..." Zagan slightly shrugged his shoulders as he responded.

"I-I'll pass that message on..." Nephteros nodded. Though, Zagan felt like he heard her mutter 'My apologies, Master Bifrons...' to herself.

"Hohoo, giving an apple to a waif whose name you don't even know. I see. My Archdemon is quite generous, isn't he?" Gremory donned an impish smile as she remarked on their exchange.

"I just did it on a whim. There isn't enough food in the world to feed every poor brat I see."

He was exaggerating, and if someone asked whether he would do it again, his honest response would be yes. However, he'd be a liar if he said he wanted to save all the world's children. Zagan wasn't a saint who cared for all the innocent people of the world. In fact, he had no qualms slugging a child who shamelessly begged him for food while acting like they deserved his charity.

"But given time, would you not receive a reward?" Gremory nodded in satisfaction as she made that claim.

"Don't be stupid. What will I ever get from some brat who's groveling on the side of the road?"

Such children didn't have much use. Their main worth was as a sacrifice, but Zagan despised sorcery that was fueled by mortal life. And frankly, taking their life over a single apple seemed unfair.

Gremory broke out into jolly laughter upon hearing Zagan's answer. And then, she spread open her mantle and spun around on the spot. When she finally came to a stop, she was about the same height as Foll. That made Zagan think she reverted to her old woman form, but…

"Keeheehee, this is the reward I was talking about…" Gremory took on the form of a ten year old girl. She had twisting goat horns, but her hands looked all squishy, and her facial features were quite tender. Plus, the way she blinked with sparkling eyes was the very definition of pure innocence. It was hard to believe that the rebellious old woman was once so charming.

Nephy and Foll clapped their hands at the sight.

"Mish Gremory, that's amazing!"

"That's so cool, Gremory. Teach me how to do that!"

"Fufu. That's right. Praise me more! I'm lauded as genius even among fomorians, so you're lucky you get to witness a display of my skill!" Gremory puffed out her chest in pride as she was showered with praise by the two girls.

How'd someone this cute turn into that old bat? Gremory had thrown Zagan for a loop, and he gradually started to doubt that this young girl and that old woman were one and the same. Setting the grim-faced Zagan aside, Gremory beckoned Nephy and Foll over to her.

"You two, lend me your ears. You listening? Mrmrmrmrmr…"

"Yes! Understood!"

"What's the point of doing that?"

Despite Foll's protests, the three of them joined hands, with Nephy at their center, and lined up in front of Zagan. And then, the three young girls they spoke in unison.

"I love you sooo much, Daddy!"

"H-Hnnngh…!"

So cute! I just want to hug them all tight! Zagan fell to his knees. That was something that had never happened, regardless of the trials he faced. Zagan stood firm when he fought against an Archangel head-on, when he came face to face with the twelve Archdemons, when he fought against the demon chimera, and even when he had the Sludge Demon Lord right before his eyes. But here he was, reduced to such a state from a single phrase.

Now that I think of it, I've never been called 'Daddy' or anything before, huh? That made sense, since Zagan's only daughter was Foll, and she only ever referred to him by name. Unfortunately, because of that, he had never experienced the destructive power of that word.

One of them was Gremory, yet he still had the urge to lovingly raise all three of them. After all, if he put in enough effort, wouldn't it be possible to raise Gremory as a quiet daughter? He was so far gone that he was even harboring such unrealistic delusions.

Nevertheless, Zagan was an Archdemon. Even as his body trembled, he stood back up.

"Hey, what are you planning... Gremory?"

"Keeheehee, don't you remember what I said? This is a reward that you can receive from children. Honest words of gratitude are quite satisfying, right?" Gremory said as she clung to his leg. Then, she laughed and smiled at him.

If it were only Gremory, then he would have just brushed her aside for being an idiot, but Nephy and Foll's presence made him want to embrace them all. It was absolutely impossible to drive them away.

"Zagan, do you want me to call you 'Daddy'?" Foll tilted her head to the side as she asked him that question.

"Erk... Well, I can't say I hate the idea..." Zagan croaked out a meek response.

"Got it. I'll practice..." Foll nodded as if she was deliberating the matter as she replied to him.

Foll was the only actual child among the three of them, which must have made her pretty confused about the whole situation... Though, that didn't mean she found it any less embarrassing. Zagan could see that her cheeks were turning red.

"Ehehe, so Mashter Zagan is my daddy, right? I thought I didn't have one…" Nephy innocently rubbed her face against Zagan's leg as she said that. And upon hearing those words, Zagan was completely taken aback.

"What do you mean, Nephy? Do you not know your parents?"

"Um, I don't really know… It's just, Mashter Zagan was the first person who held my hand and treated me nice like a parent would…"

Did Nephy currently only have memories from when she was around five years old? That would add up, since she was persecuted at the time, but her not even knowing her parents felt weird. She clearly understood the concept of parental relations and families, so her not knowing must have meant she'd never even met them. And while Zagan ruminated over that fact, Nephy looked up at him anxiously.

"Did I… say something bad again?"

"No, not at all. Have I ever even scolded you before?" Zagan lined up his sight with Nephy's by going down on one knee, then spoke as if admonishing her. And, as the tips of Nephy's ears quivered happily, she wrapped her arms around his neck and pulled him into an embrace.

"Mashter Zagan, I love you so much!"

Zagan brushed her hair as he thought over what she'd said mere moments ago.

"Did I… say something bad again?" He felt that wasn't a statement a small child should repeat so often.

It's probably something she got used to saying because she blamed herself for how the other elves treated her… In other words, Nephy had reverted to her default mannerisms from back then. The reason she could smile constantly was because this was before she shut her heart away for good.

Why am I hated? What do I have to do to get everyone to like me? Back then, she surely harbored such thoughts. And if she were to grow up under Zagan's care from that day forward, Nephy may have been able to live without the burden of her more painful memories. After all, even Zagan's childhood memories had grown fuzzy by the time he was a teen.

"Little Nephy, children don't do anything bad. They simply do the wrong things when they aren't taught properly. That's why there's nothing for you to be afraid of here…" Kimaris squatted down in front of Nephy and smiled at her as he said that. Maybe he had come to the same conclusion as Zagan.

"…Really?"

"Of course."

"Then, is it okay for me to ask for something selfish?" Nephy pleaded with him while twiddling her fingers together, and Kimaris smiled right back at her.

"By all means, ask for anything you want."

Nephy's face brightened up due to his response. And then, she spoke to him with a grand smile on her face.

"Can I… ruffle up your mane, Shir Kimry?"

"Ruffle…?" Kimaris stared back at her in wonder. He had never in his wildest dreams expected such a request.

"I guess… I can't?"

"No, I do not mind. Go right ahead."

"Yaaaay, thank you! I love Shir Kimry, too!" Nephy said as she began ruffling his mane. Then, she brushed it all the way up to his chin, which made Kimaris let out a voice that was a mix of happiness and embarrassment.

"I'll… have to remain in my beast form for a while huh?"

"Sorry, Kimaris…" Zagan thought back on it, and he quickly realized that Kimaris spent a lot of time in the castle in his lion form. He always assumed that was because Foll had liked it, but maybe Kimaris just enjoyed spending time with children.

"The hell are you former Archdemon candidates doing? This ain't the time to goof off with brats! Don't you remember the situation we're in?" Barbatos chastised them with a snort.

"Shir Boboto, are you angry?" Nephy made a surprised face upon hearing his complaints.

"It's Barbatos."

"Yes, Shir Boboto."

"Ugh… Whatever, that's fine," Barbatos said, giving up on correcting her. It seemed his name was quite difficult to pronounce.

Haven't you mellowed out, too? Perhaps he was just lonely because nobody was paying attention to him. Barbatos' reaction was so underwhelming that his true feelings were called into doubt. And even as he grimaced, he squatted down in front of Nephy.

"You hear me, you lil' brat? Seems like Zagan can't act all tough in front of you. Now's the time to be selfish and cause him all sorts of trouble, you hear?"

"You can't trouble Mashter Zagan!"

"Oh, come on, didn't that lion there tell you to ask for whatever you want? Brats like you exist to trouble adults. And hey, I bet that guy'll be happier if you do. Right? Don't you also want to make Zagan happi— Erk?" Zagan mercilessly drove his fist into the head of the villain who was attempting to corrupt such a pure girl.

"Hear me, Nephy. Do not follow the words of suspicious adults, okay?"

"Yes, Mashter Zagan! But isn't Shir Boboto also a good person?"

125

"I'm not so sure about that..." Zagan glared at Barbatos, who let out an uncomfortable snort as he said that. And while all that was going on, Nephteros finally recovered from her unrest, and she let out a sigh.

"All of you... really are taking it easy, huh?" Nephteros was likely just talking to herself, but upon hearing that, Gremory formed a broad grin.

"Hey, Big Sis, play with meee!"

"Play!" Foll jumped up and embraced her, following Gremory's lead.

"Ah, h-hey, what are you doing? Cut it out!" Nephteros protested.

"Big Shish, please play with me!" Nephy finally chimed in as she joined the other two girls.

"Erk, you little..." Nephteros wanted to protest again, but she remembered that being cold to Nephy had reduced her to tears mere moments ago. And though she looked extremely conflicted about the matter, she eventually slumped her shoulders to signal her resignation.

"...Well, what do you want to do?"

"Let's play tag!"

"Let's go sing!"

"Let's go pick flowers!"

"Narrow it down a little!" Nephteros quipped back at them in anger, which made the three little girls giggle. Though, she wasn't actually all that mad. Sure, there was a bitter expression on her face, but she actually wanted to spend time with them.

"What's going on here?" Chastille remarked as she walked out of the elder's manor.

Gremory had transformed into a little girl, Kimaris was being used as a chair by three little girls, Barbatos had collapsed, and Nephteros was playing around with them.

Considering Chastille's perspective of things, this was a truly messed up situation. However, Zagan simply shook his head like it was no big deal.

"Everyone needs a little downtime once in a while."

"Downtime, you say? Aren't we in danger right now?"

"Oh, no. Don't worry. We're perfectly safe. I'll just blow this village to smithereens when we want to get out of this barrier," Zagan remarked casually.

"Y-You're going to blow it up...? Isn't this Nephy's hometown?"

"And...? Well, just think of that as our last resort. More importantly, did you find anything?" Zagan had called her back earlier, but Chastille continued her investigation of the manor instead of responding to his call. That had to mean something.

"Yeah." Chastille said with a nod. Then, she continued by saying, "I found a hidden compartment in the village elder's room. And this is what I found stored inside..." Chastille pulled a single book out from behind her back. It was handwritten, just like the village journals, but upon seeing the title, Zagan squinted his eyes.

"Do you understand the meaning of the words on the cover?"

"No, I can't read the elven language... Is it something important?"

"Well, yeah..." Zagan was excited by the sight. And of course he was, since it was exactly what he had been looking for. Still, he wondered whether it was really alright for him to look through the contents. He agonized over that decision but finally decided he could not pass up on the clue Chastille had found. This was no time to hesitate. And so, Zagan accepted the journal.

"Was this book the only thing you found?"

"No, this was hidden alongside it…" Chastille held up a single pendant as she said that. Though, perhaps pendant wasn't a suitable word. It looked more like an arrowhead that had been strung up. It wasn't all that large, but it had ten jewels set in its surface and a crest like that of a tree carved into it.

"It's not a crest used for sorcery, but I've seen this before. If I remember correctly, it's called the 'Tree of Life,' and it is a symbol that represents Celestian… You found that beside this journal?" Zagan nodded deeply as he questioned Chastille.

"Yeah. It looks like an antique, but I can't tell what it's worth," Chastille replied, nodding right back at Zagan.

"Why don't you just hand that over to me…"

"Oh, okay…"

It looked to be made of silver, but that wasn't the case. The thing was endowed with frighteningly powerful mana, and tapping it with his nail was enough to convince Zagan that it was far sturdier than any normal sword. It was so strong that it almost felt as if it was made by kneading together mana itself…

"Is this mithril?"

"Mithril, you say? You mean the substance that's said to be on the same level as the metal gods use in legends, orichalcum?"

"Yeah. This is the first time I've seen the real thing. Should've known a hidden elven village would have some lying around."

"Hey, wait, is that seriously mithril!?" Barbatos shot up to his feet as soon as he heard them discussing the rare substance.

"Shut it. This likely belongs to Nephy," Zagan declared. Though, he had to be careful, as someone could have booby-trapped it.

Guess I'll figure out whether it's dangerous before handing it over to Nephy.

"Oh, come on, at least let me take a look! Actually, where the hell'd you even find that thing?"

"I found it. At least question the right person!" Chastille said with an exasperated expression on her face.

"H-Hey, Zagan? She's... her, right? That crybaby, I mean..." Barbatos looked completely taken aback by Chastille's words.

"Yeah, that's her, alright."

"Man, this barrier must be rewriting the laws of the universe! That's the only way to explain her actually being useful for a change."

"How dare you... Don't you think you're going too far?"

"And she's not bawling her eyes out even though I insulted her!?" Barbatos fell to his knees, acting as if something beyond his comprehension had occurred.

"I'm in the middle of my professional duties right now. Say, don't you think it's about time you get serious? I don't hate being teased, but there's a time and place for everything," Chastille claimed.

She actually enjoys being teased? Zagan couldn't believe his ears, but her words seemed to shock Barbatos even more.

"I-I don't believe it! What's this feeling? Am I... trembling?" Barbatos was grumbling and muttering to himself repeatedly in a conflicted manner. He seemed troubled by his newfound knowledge of Chastille's feelings.

"I'm going to look into these. I'll leave Nephy and the others to you," Zagan said as he stood up and looked over to Chastille.

"That's fine by me, but tell me one thing before you go. You can read the elven language, right?"

"Yeah. And?"

"What's the title of that book?" Chastille replied in a dignified tone.

Zagan was startled by her question, but he quickly regained his composure and decided that she deserved an explanation after going through the trouble of finding it.

"'Nephilim.' It means one who fell from heaven. I think... it's the root of Nephy's name."

In other words, Chastille had found a journal about Nephy.

The journal began with the following preface.

Nowadays, there are none but I who know of this fact, but there was once a devil within this village. The devil left the village long ago, but just once, it returned for a single day. And when it did, the devil left behind a baby. That child may well be the harbinger of calamity, which is why I'm documenting all this information. If the devil truly returns one day, I pray that this aids you in vanquishing it.

—Month of the Dragon, Day of Water.

Something terrifying happened. That devil returned to the village.

It's all that damn repulsive, cursed child's fault. What manner of trouble will befall this village next?

When I was a child, that devil was already a calamity that ate away at this village like a parasite. Many of my brethren lost their lives when they were used as sacrifices or test subjects.

I feel like I can still hear them when I close my eyes. There hasn't been a single day where their screams cease. They run through my mind, haunting me endlessly.

How dare that devil bring a baby to this village! Sure, it told me that I may boil or burn that baby as I pleased before leaving, but this is all far too suspicious.

The baby was carrying a mithril pendant modeled after the Tree of Life. It seemed to be quite a work of art, but I did not know its true nature, so I confiscated it.

I knew the baby bore no sin, but it was also clear to me that the child could grow to become another devil. I hesitated as I mulled over what to do, but I eventually decided to kill the baby.

This was for the greater good. As much as I hated it, I had to act in the best interest of our village.

However, I couldn't kill it. That thing was already a devil. The trees of the forest rushed in at me as if they possessed a will of their own, tearing off the arm with a blade in it.

What a terrifying child. I thought of trying to starve it, but the forest still kept it alive regardless.

I came to realize we possessed no means of killing that thing, so I entrusted the baby over to the village's most skilled archers, the Neruel household. I felt sorry for them, but in the worst case scenario, they were the only ones who possessed enough power to protect themselves.

—omitted—

—Month of the Lion, Day of Fire.

It has been five years since the cursed child's arrival.

The thing's growing rather quickly. The Neruels have confined it to the cellar, but when it emerges from time to time, there's always an eerie smile on its face. It's repulsive.

The people of the village raised concerns as to whether that thing should be chained down, but I knew it was meaningless to bind it.

I rejected them at that time by saying that doing such a thing would be unjust, but it was plain as day that my decision invited dissatisfaction.

Perhaps the only good fortune is the fact that the forest has been silent since I lost my arm. Thanks to that, the veil of fear over the village is thin.

This is surely the boon of putting out a strict order that it was not to be harmed. Everyone's happy because they think it doesn't possess any power.

Yes, I didn't even tell the Neruels how I lost my arm. Nobody else needs to know of that nightmare.

Even though the people of the village hate it, they don't appear to fear it. It's fine for them not to know that it's a devil with enough power to wipe out our village in a single breath. They'll be happier that way. My only remaining concern is how long that thing will remain docile...

—omitted—

—Month of the Sylph, Day of Earth.

It has been ten years since the cursed child's arrival.

It no longer comes outside, and that eerie smile has disappeared. The people of the village have stopped caring about its existence, and the Neruels' burden seems to have lightened considerably.

It's good that it's peaceful, but I can't relax. I recently found the corpse of a strange bird right near the village.

It's likely a sorcerer's familiar. And this is the third one that's turned up in the Month of the Sylph.

Something from the outside may be trying to invade our village. And when I think of that, the devil comes to mind.

Perhaps now that the cursed child has grown, it's coming to pick it back up? Well, I can speculate all I want, but I have no way of knowing what its true intentions are.

Is this the result that devil desired? Or did it not go as it willed? I don't know. However, I do know that a tremendous calamity will befall us in the near future.

I cannot allow that to happen. But, I also believe... there's the option of having the cursed child clash with the devil...

◇

"...I can't even bear looking at this..." Zagan shut the book, which even managed to make him feel nauseous, after finishing it. He was currently in the village elder's room. The journal wasn't all that long, and he finished reading all of it in but a single minute.

The author was clearly the elder, and it detailed how Nephy had become the despondent girl he first met. It was all because no one ever realized that the little girl showed her pure smile in hopes of getting along with people.

Seems that lovely smile looked eerie to them because of their paranoia.

Well, that may have been reasonable, considering their first meeting ended with an arm being lost, but the elder was simply getting what they deserved for trying to kill Nephy in the first place.

As Zagan let out a single sigh, he threw the journal into the air. And without a sound, it turned to ash and crumbled before hitting the floor. He felt sorry for Chastille, who went out of her way to find it, but Zagan didn't want Nephy ever seeing it. Besides, he could memorize the contents of a book completely by just reading it once, so there was no need to leave such an unpleasant thing laying around.

Shall I reduce this village to ash after we finish our investigation? At first, Zagan thought to wait until Nephy managed to sort out her

133

feelings, but he no longer felt like that was a good idea. Though, he had no intention of saying that it was for Nephy's sake or anything. If he were to use such an excuse, he would be no different from the one who wrote that journal. Sorcerers like him loathed people who claimed to act for the greater good.

Zagan didn't like it at all, and he couldn't forgive them, so the only option left was to erase them. Even if they were already dead, he would eliminate every last trace.

Zagan found Chastille and Barbatos waiting for him as he exited the elder's manor. It seemed that they were curious about the contents of the journal. And, as the two of them looked at Zagan's face, they shrank back with a start.

"H-Hey... You already done reading? So, what was with that book?" Barbatos asked.

"It's ash now."

"Huh?" Barbatos was at a complete loss for words, and Chastille had a worried expression on her face.

"It's probably better... not to ask what was written in it, huh?"

"Well, I managed to find several clues in it, at least," Zagan responded, shrugging his shoulders like it was no big deal.

"Clues?" Chastille tilted her head to the side, which elicited a nod from Zagan.

"Seems Nephy wasn't born in this village. An abandoned child... No, that's not quite right, but it seems she was brought to this village when she was a baby. And on top of that, the one who dropped her off was considered a devil by this village, which was why they all mistreated her."

Oddly enough, Chastille smiled in relief upon hearing those words.

"I see. That's good news, then."

"…How?" Zagan unintentionally replied in a critical tone, which made Chastille nod.

"That means Nephy's real family wasn't part of this village, right? I don't know if it will make her feel better, but the fact that her family may still be alive is good news, isn't it?"

"I'm surprised you can think of it that way. I mean, even if they are alive, that just means they abandoned her, right?" Zagan stared back at her in wonder as he replied.

In response, Chastille blinked back in a daze, as if saying, 'Huh, you're one to talk.'

"Even you tried to keep Nephy at a distance once, didn't you? Why was that?" Chastille responded in a matter-of-fact manner.

Zagan had once hurt Nephy and kept her at a distance. That was because he felt fear upon meeting the twelve Archdemons. Back then, he knew he would eventually become an ally of those monsters. However, he wished to spare Nephy such a fate. Zagan wanted Nephy to live under the light of day. It was a foolish thought brought on by his own weakness. After all, a real man would protect absolutely everything dear to him, including Nephy herself.

In other words, she's trying to say that Nephy's parents might have also made the same mistake…? Zagan unintentionally formed a bitter smile.

"That's quite an optimistic view."

"Looking at the way all of you are, I want to believe that's the case…" Chastille's levelheaded opinion was completely unusual. It was throwing everyone present for a loop.

"Huh? Aren't you gonna track them down and get revenge?" Barbatos said as he knit his brows.

"…Why do you only ever have such disgusting ideas?"

"The hell do you think sorcerers are?"

Zagan felt strangely relieved as he watched the two of them squabble.

These two actually complement each other, don't they? Honestly, it felt like they were skillfully keeping up a balancing act. And at the same time, Zagan realized that the anger he had been harboring since reading the journal was thinning out.

"Well, I guess I'll limit it to just blowing up the elder's manor, then."

"Why even bother?" Barbatos inquired.

"As a distraction, I guess?" Zagan replied resolutely. Barbatos was left dumbfounded. And Chastille let out an amused laugh from right next to him.

"Cracking jokes already, huh? Must mean you're back to normal now."

"Huh...? I wasn't making a joke, though."

"What? It... wasn't a joke?" Chastille was shocked for some reason, but Zagan felt like he understood what she was trying to say.

I made her worry about me? Well, Zagan was aware that he must have seemed on edge, so perhaps Chastille's desire to comfort him made sense.

Even though she's usually such a useless crybaby, she knows when to get serious. At the very least, she did once fight Zagan on even grounds.

"There was one other clue in the journal. It's probable that the 'devil' or whatever from the journal is the one who attacked Nephy."

"Huh...? Hold on. If that's true, then wouldn't that 'devil' or whatever be Nephy's relative?"

"The possibility exists, but I don't have any proof. For all we know, she was abducted as a baby, right?"

"That's... true..." Chastille nodded without refuting his statement at all.

"But then, why's that guy the culprit?" Barbatos tilted his head to the side as he questioned Zagan.

"The process of elimination. There are almost no other suspects when it comes to people who can come and go from a hidden village that even the Archdemons didn't know existed. Plus, they have to be an elf too. The 'devil' the journal spoke of was definitely a native."

"Hm... The only famous elven sorcerer that comes to mind is 'Fairy Queen' Titania," Barbatos said as he stroked his chin, looking deep in thought. Zagan had also heard that name before.

"You mean the elf who challenged Archdemon Orias and lost?"

Archdemon Orias was still alive. In fact, that particular Archdemon should have been at the gathering where Zagan joined their ranks.

"Yeah. Titania was hellbent on creating an elven country, so she led an army of familiars using elven sorcery and picked a fight with Orias. That's still considered to be the greatest battle against Archdemons in history."

It definitely wouldn't have been difficult for such a skilled elf to turn Nephy into a child or form the barrier that wrapped around the village. However, Zagan shook his head.

"Didn't Titania die several hundred years ago?"

"Yeah, but I've never even heard of any other elven sorcerers. Most of them keep their identities secret, since they get killed when they're found out."

It was the same as Foll hiding the fact that she was a dragon. Elves were used as sacrifices and catalysts, and even a single strand of hair or a single drop of blood had extraordinary value. Enough value that it was worth staring death in the eyes to get a meager amount.

Sorcerer or not, there were countless people who wanted to get their hands on them. And because of that, an elven sorcerer would never unveil their identity.

Guess I'll try contacting Orias once we get out of here... Zagan didn't really want to, but that Archdemon seemed familiar with elven sorcerers. And if they were perhaps involved in their current predicament, it would be fine to kill them in response. There was no changing the fact that Zagan was pissed, after all.

"Well, I can hunt down the culprit whenever I want. More importantly, how are Nephy and the others doing?" Zagan asked as he pulled himself out of his murderous thoughts.

"If you're looking for Nephy, she's over there," Chastille said, pointing over to the plaza in the middle of the village. And as he looked over, Zagan spotted three young girls leaning against Kimaris in his lion form.

"Hmm. So she's asleep."

Chastille and Barbatos returned to the manor to gather any valuables before Zagan blew them to bits. It wasn't like he planned to destroy it right away, but he was glad that they were getting it ready ahead of time, so he didn't stop them.

Kimaris was curled up under a large tree in the middle of the village, and the three little girls next to him were all sound asleep. Nephteros was sitting down next to them, hugging her knees. It seemed she was quite worn out, as she looked thoroughly exhausted.

"...Hey, that's your family over there, right? Why do I have to be their babysitter?" Nephteros questioned Zagan with a pointed glare on her face. If she was aware that she had been stuck on babysitting

duty, it would have been fine for her to just run away, but she remained regardless.

"Well, sorry about that. You have my thanks," Zagan responded, which made Nephteros stare back in wonder.

"I've thought this for quite a while now, but you really are an atypical Archdemon, huh?"

"I've been trying to act more arrogant and audacious, though…"

"A truly arrogant person wouldn't offer their thanks to people."

Zagan simply shrugged his shoulders as he realized Nephteros had a point. And then, he looked over to the little girls who appeared to be sleeping comfortably.

They all look so cute when they're asleep… Nephy and Foll were already angels, but even Gremory looked adorable, which amazed him. And, as he gazed over them with a charmed expression, Nephteros looked up at Zagan like she had something to say.

"What? Got something to say?"

"Not really. It's not like I'm complaining or anything, but…"

"If there's something on your mind, then try talking about it. You never know, it could come in handy in this situation," Zagan claimed in an attempt to ease Nephteros' tension. He planned to say that in as gentle a tone as possible, but it wasn't like just anybody other than Nephy could read his words well, so he just had to hope for the best.

"It has nothing to do with this village at all, though…" Nephteros opened her mouth to speak, seemingly still on edge.

"I don't mind. Speak," Zagan gently urged. Emboldened by his words, Nephteros timidly began speaking.

"Do you… remember when you were about the same age as these children?"

That was a completely random question, so Nephteros' attempt to avoid asking it made sense.

"Let's see. Everything I can recall is quite worthless, but I do remember them, yes," Zagan replied, nodding back toward Nephteros despite his confusion.

"...For example?"

"Like when I failed to run away after stealing food and nearly got beaten to death, or when I spent an entire week without eating anything and managed to find some moldy bread, but was left loitering around on the border of death due to disease, or when I got lured by food from a sorcerer, was abducted, and was nearly used as a sacrifice. Stuff like that, basically..." Zagan tried talking about various memories, but all of them ended up pointing back to food in the end. How embarrassing.

"Is only having memories of near-death experiences normal?"

"Hm... Well, I had so many of those experiences that I simply had to become a sorcerer. I guess that's probably not normal at all, huh?" Zagan realized nothing about that was normal, but there was nobody around to point that out.

"Can I... talk about something a little weird?" Nephteros asked as she continued to languidly hug her knees.

"Go ahead," Zagan instantly replied. He could tell that she was worried about something. Setting aside whether he could actually give her any advice, Zagan knew that he could at least hear her out. And upon being told to go ahead, Nephteros began speaking in a frightened voice.

"I don't... remember anything from when I was their age."

"You mean you lost your memories?" Zagan asked as he raised a brow.

"...I don't know. To be honest, I never even thought about it until now."

Serving under an Archdemon didn't provide any opportunities to get involved with children, so perhaps that was only natural.

"And also, why does Nephy have the same face as me...?"

Zagan was actually the one who wanted to ask that question, but it seemed she didn't know the answer herself.

"Who am I...?" Nephteros said in a trembling voice, sounding ready to burst into tears at any moment.

Ask someone like Chastille, not me... Zagan wasn't even any good at comforting Nephy. He had no clue what to say at times like this. And so, after worrying about it for a while, he simply snorted in a bored tone.

"How worthless."

"..." Nephteros silently slumped her shoulders as Zagan continued speaking.

"What kind of answer do you expect? Frankly, even I don't know who I am or where I was born. But still, aren't I just me? I mean, how can a person ever be anyone other than who they are in the moment?"

Nephteros stared at Zagan with a blank expression on her face. She was left confused, unsure whether he was making fun of her or

admonishing her, and before long, she opened her mouth to try to figure out what was going on.

"Could it be… Are you trying to comfort me?"

"Take it however you will," Zagan replied nonchalantly. However, in the next instant, he opened his eyes wide in surprise. He was stunned by the sight of Nephteros' mouth loosening up and forming a gentle smile.

"I see. I feel like I finally understand why Nephelia said that the way you worry about things is cute."

"…Do you think I won't kill you just because you're a guest?" Zagan grimaced as he responded in a clearly agitated tone.

"For the time being, I suppose I should offer my thanks. I feel… just a little better now," Nephteros said as she stood up with a bitter smile on her face. Zagan found her expression of gratitude quite embarrassing, so all he did was shrug his shoulders.

"By the way, what's that?" Nephteros knit her brows as she questioned Zagan.

"What do you mean…? Oh, this?" Zagan exclaimed as he realized Nephteros was pointing at the mithril pendant. It was the one that was found alongside the journal about Nephy. Before he knew it, the chain had spilled out of his pocket, and it was dangling about.

Now that I think of it, I haven't examined this thing yet… Zagan took the pendant out of his pocket as he realized his mistake.

"It was hidden in the elder's manor. I haven't looked into it yet, but it seems to have some mechanism binding it."

"Really? Can I take a look?"

"I don't mind, but don't break it, okay?"

"I won't," Nephteros responded in an exasperated tone. Then, she took the pendant and began examining it, and after a while she raised a brow.

"It looks like it opens up here. Are you sure it's locked?"

"What, really?" Zagan took a closer look at the pendant as that fact was pointed out to him. That was when he noticed that the pendant had a small gap in it.

"Can you open it?"

"I'll give it a try…" Nephteros said as she tried picking at it with her nails a few times. Eventually, she seemed to find a clasp and pressed into it, which opened the pendant with a click. And inside, there was a single portrait and a short inscription.

"Is this… Nephy and her mother?"

The portrait was a painting of a baby with white hair being embraced by a young female elf. The older woman was likely Nephy's mother, as they resembled each other. She also possessed white hair and azure eyes… which could only mean she was a high elf.

This wasn't all that surprising, but the inscription posed a huge problem. Stunned by the sight, Zagan read it aloud in hopes of being corrected.

"To my beloved daughter, Nephelia — Titania."

That was the name of the elf who had challenged Archdemon Orias hundreds of years ago and perished as a result.

"Titania... huh?" Zagan muttered as he held up the pendant that Nephteros opened earlier.

It was evening now, they had already finished dinner, and Nephy and Foll were chatting in front of the fireplace with acorns spread out before them. The acorns that Zagan baked that night on impulse were unexpectedly popular. He had used honey to cover up the fact that they didn't really have any seasoning, but it seemed their curiosity made them forget about the bland taste.

Barbatos was practically drowning himself in liquor at a nearby table, and Chastille was attempting to stop him. Nephteros was in another chair, lost in thought over something while gazing at the fireplace. She was somewhat anxious due to what they discussed during the afternoon, but it did look like she had almost fully recovered. If it were to drag on more, then Zagan would have been forced to take care of her at his castle for a while.

Kimaris and Gremory weren't around. After a serious round of rock-paper-scissors, it was decided that cleaning up after dinner would be left to them. And so, they were stuck washing the tableware while complaining about how cramped the kitchen was.

After checking on the condition of his companions, Zagan let out a sigh. *What do I do?*

There wasn't much in terms of buildings worth mentioning left in the village. And because Barbatos and the others had investigated

them all during the day, all notable books and goods were already gathered before him. All that was really left was to somehow escape and turn Nephy back to normal.

However, Zagan was worried about two things. First was the name inscribed within the pendant, Titania. This sorcerer was said to have passed away several hundred years ago, but the pendant indicated that Nephy was her daughter. In other words, Nephy was the daughter of Titania, but the discrepancy in time made no sense. After all, she battled an Archdemon. The chances of Titania surviving for so long after that without anyone knowing were rather slim. Archdemons generally weren't interested in others, but they showed no mercy or sympathy for their enemies.

There was always the chance that Orias captured her, but in that case, she would have been used as a sacrifice or a test subject. Zagan was sure she would never have had an opportunity to be blessed with a child, or the stamina to give birth to one, under those circumstances.

Though, there was always the possibility that Orias was like Zagan and fell in love with Titania at first sight. Unfortunately, none of the Archdemons seemed all that kind. And with that ruled out, there was only one remaining possibility, but…

If I'm right, killing Orias might be a bad idea… There was an eighty or ninety percent chance that the culprit this time around was Orias. Their connection to Titania would have lead to them learning of this village. They must have turned Nephy into a child so that she could learn to harness her power from a young age. According to Chastille, the aura in this village was strong. Moreover, it lent its power to Nephy with little effort on her part. Even several Archdemon candidates gathered together would have trouble placing a curse on her at the moment.

Zagan thought about his predicament, realizing it would be difficult for him to bring down someone on his level without lethal force. Plus, would defeating Orias even be enough to return Nephy to normal? There were many issues that plagued his thoughts when he thought of his first problem. As for the other problem...

Zagan cast his gaze over to Foll and Nephy, who were smiling at each other. Nephy's emotions were usually readily apparent due to the movement of her ears, but it was very rare for anything to show on her face. She likely could not do it due to her upbringing, but Zagan felt like her facial muscles were gradually loosening as time passed.

Still, this was the first time Zagan saw her smiling brightly. The direct cause of Nephy becoming expressionless was obviously the trauma of being abandoned in this village. However, the way the elves mistreated her also played a clear part. After flipping through the elder's journal, Zagan could understand why Nephy lost her smile.

Now then, between this Nephy and the real Nephy, which of the two is happier? This young girl was still Nephy. She still possessed the desire to comfort those who were troubled, even as a child. And it wasn't like she lost all memories of the time she spent with Zagan and the others.

Above all else, Zagan wanted to protect Nephy's smile, and he knew returning her to normal would make it disappear. Sorcerers lived long lives. Given another ten or so years, Nephy would grow back to her prior state, so there was also the option of just waiting it out. Ten years were practically nothing to him, and that way, she could preserve her smile.

After seeing the heart-wrenching contents of that journal, he couldn't help but want to wait. And while Zagan was racking his

brains over the matter, Gremory and Kimaris returned from the kitchen. It seemed that it was troublesome to revert her age, so Gremory was still in the form of a little girl. Also, Kimaris took on his lion form in order to entertain the girls.

"We've finished with cleaning up," Gremory reported.

"Oh, good work."

"Huh…? What's that? You're making an awfully troubled face there. Is it really that difficult to break through the barrier around the village?" Gremory asked. Zagan realized he must have been making quite the expression for Gremory to pay him consideration.

"Do you know of Archdemon Orias?" Zagan inquired, shrugging his shoulders as he held up the pendant.

"W-Well, I at least know the name… Could it be…?" Gremory's face spasmed as she spat out an answer.

"Yeah, Orias probably caused all this. So, I've been worrying about whether to kill them."

"Ah… Like I thought…" Gremory put her hand to her face, losing herself in thought upon hearing his response.

"What? Is it someone you know?"

"Ah… Umm…" Gremory stumbled over her words as she desperately searched for an answer.

"Archdemon Orias is Miss Gremory's teacher," Kimaris cut in, answering in Gremory's stead.

"Really?" Zagan exclaimed, nearly dropping the pendant as he heard that.

"…Umm, yeah…" Gremory nervously muttered.

"You… noticed it was Orias already, didn't you?" Zagan stated as he watched the sweat pour down her brow.

"I just thought… it might be the case."

Well, Gremory's sorcery and the curse cast on Nephy had many things in common. Noticing the connection should have been simple, but Zagan was distracted by Nephy turning into a child, which made him overlook it.

"Let me just say this now, I didn't know anything about this, okay? It's been almost a hundred years since I last met Orias. Oh, and I didn't leak any information, either," Gremory claimed as she waved her hands about in a fluster.

"It's not like I'm questioning you about any wrongdoings," Zagan said. He understood why Gremory kept that information to herself. If it was known that someone related to the culprit was within the sealed space, they would instantly be labeled an enemy. That was why he had no intention of criticizing her for her actions. Instead, Zagan threw her a question.

"What kind of sorcerer is Orias?"

"Let's see… The sorcery I use to manipulate my age is something I learned from my teacher, so Orias can use the same thing. Also… Ah, that's right, my teacher is most likely an elf."

"…Are you certain?"

"Yeah. Orias always wore a hood, so I never even saw their face, but I did catch sight of what was below it just once. The ears were unmistakably those of an elf."

"I see…" Zagan responded.

"But, Sir Orias is said to have killed Fairy Queen Titania, right? Would another elf really do something like that?" Kimaris asked in a puzzled tone.

"…Isn't it natural for elves to discriminate against their own kind?" Zagan knew that sounded harsh, but reading about how Nephy was treated by the villagers had angered him.

Kimaris groaned in response, like he wasn't at all convinced, but Zagan simply nodded.

"It all makes sense now. You have my thanks," Zagan said, expressing his gratitude.

"What's that? You're not going to get angry and say I should've told you sooner?" Gremory asked as she stared back at him in wonder.

"I'm the idiot for not noticing sooner. It's not like it's your fault or anything."

"This form of mine seems to be quite convenient in front of my Archdemon, huh?" Gremory remarked as she looked down at her own childish figure.

"...Let me just say, I'm more than willing to kill children if they make themselves my enemy."

"Keeheehee, I'll tread lightly, then," Gremory laughed pleasantly as she left to join Foll and Nephy in front of the fireplace. And even while glaring at her in an annoyed manner, he nodded slightly.

With this, I know how to deal with Orias... The only remaining problem was Nephy. As Zagan began groaning while gazing at the pendant, someone tugged on the hem of his robe. Turning to look at them, he noticed that Nephy had suddenly come up next to him with a worried expression on her face.

"Nephy? Shouldn't you be playing with Gremory and Foll?"

"Mashter Zagan, did something happen? You're making a very troubled face..." Nephy asked as she shook her head energetically to deny his question. In the end, this child really was Nephy. It seemed there was no way he could keep any secrets from her. And so, Zagan nodded as he resigned himself to his fate.

"Let's see... Nephy, if something bad were to happen and you had the chance to do it over, what would you do?"

It wasn't like he was entrusting the answer to the problem to Nephy herself, but he at least wanted to hear her thoughts.

"Doing it over... means it never happened in the first place, right?" Nephy asked.

"That's right. To make it so it never happened, and do it all over again."

With that, Nephy began puzzling over it deeply with a cute moan as if she was faced with a difficult problem. *I see. The figure of someone worrying over things can be quite adorable, huh?* Zagan highly doubted that he looked anywhere near as cute, but he at least thought that Nephy had a point. And before long, Nephy began putting her thoughts into words.

"Today, when I was looking for acorns with Big Shish Foll, I got really scared when I saw some bugs."

When he thought back on it, Zagan remembered hearing Nephy let out a scream while she was out gathering acorns. It seemed she panicked upon picking up one that was being eaten by insects. Zagan made a mental note to burn that acorn to ash later.

"I didn't like that, but if I made it so it never happened, wouldn't that mean I didn't go to gather acorns with Big Shish Foll? I think... I'd like that even less."

"Even if you were still able to go gather acorns with Foll?"

"Yeah... I mean, when I was about to cry, Big Shish Foll took the acorn and threw it really far away to cheer me up. Isn't that something I saw because I went through something bad?"

Upon seeing Nephy do her best to answer him, Zagan hoisted her up and set her down on his lap. And as he did, Nephy happily smiled with an 'Ehehe.'

"I see. It's just as you say. Even painful memories are formative experiences."

"Yes!" Nephy answered him with a huge grin on her face.

"Remember how you said you love me, Nephy? Well, I feel the same way about you. But, in the end, I think that includes everything, from the painful memories we share to the road we've walked together..." Zagan stated in a grave tone.

This wasn't just about the matters at the hidden village. It was also about when Zagan hurt her, and even about when she was hurt by Nephteros. Despite all the issues, those moments they spent together were precious memories to Zagan. And so, as he gently brushed her head while talking, Nephy looked back at him curiously.

"Nephy, I love you. That's why I'll bring back the Nephy that I love," Zagan declared. He'd finally found his answer, so he continued by saying, "From here on out, you will surely experience more painful memories. But, you will always have a place to belong by my side. That's why, um, how do I put it..."

Nephy listened carefully, her full attention on Zagan as he struggled to find the words to convey his feelings. And as he grew conscious of that fact, Zagan struggled all the more. Still, he eventually finished what he was saying without faltering.

"Could you stay with... No, that's a little wrong. Stay with me, Nephy. You are mine. That's why... from now on, I won't allow anyone to meddle with you, and won't allow you to lose anything."

It was surely a difficult topic for Nephy to understand as she was now. The little Nephy stared back at him in wonder for a moment, but nodded soon after.

"Yes! I'll follow Mashter Zagan anywhere!"

"...Good girl."

After he brushed her head one more time, Nephy got off his lap. And, after stretching out lightly, Zagan called out to the others in the room.

"You guys, it's about time to blow this place away. Get ready to go home."

"HUH!?"

Every single one of them let out a dumbfounded voice.

"You mean now? It's already dark out!" Barbatos was whining like he still wanted to knock back some more drinks, but Zagan paid him no mind.

"If you fancy the liquor, then just bring it back with you. I'll wait thirty minutes, so be quick about it."

"Zagan, I'm sleepy…" Foll came up to him while rubbing her eyes.

"Then get some sleep. Kimaris, I'll leave Foll and Nephy to you."

"As you wish," Kimaris replied, as he placed Foll on his back with a strained smile on his face.

"My goodness, where exactly did that troubled expression of yours go?" Gremory called out to Zagan in an exasperated tone.

"It was just a momentary lapse in judgment. Don't worry about it."

Leaving it at that, Gremory began gathering books, bows, and all sorts of goods of interest with her little body.

"You sure brought that up suddenly, didn't you? Is there a reason to hurry up now?" Nephteros muttered in a surprised tone.

"There's no real reason to hurry, but I don't have any reason to stay under observation any longer, either."

Orias was likely still nearby and observing the state of Zagan's group. Since Zagan had decided on a course of action, there was no longer any need to just go with the flow.

"Seems you've finally returned to your usual self, huh?" Chastille said in a curious tone.

"Have I?"

"Yeah. So, what should I do?"

"Protect Nephy and Foll. That's more than enough," Zagan proclaimed as he brushed Nephy's head.

"I'll take care of everything else myself."

No matter who his opponent was, no matter what expectations they had, the fact that they meddled with Nephy was an unshakable truth. As such, Zagan had to be the one to bring the hammer down on them.

Upon going outside, the group noticed that the air was warm. They had finished gathering everything necessary together, and all members were now present at the plaza in front of the manor. They didn't know what was going to happen from here, so Gremory quit playing around and took on her adult form.

"So, what's the plan? I thought you couldn't devour this barrier?" Barbatos asked, which elicited a nod from Zagan.

"Be it sorcery or mysticism, mana or aura, there's no changing the fact that the flow of the power is being manipulated. If that is burned to ash, then a mere barrier won't be able to maintain itself."

"Huh...? I don't really understand the theory behind sorcery, but is it fine to do such a thing? Aura is the power of nature itself, you know?" Chastille tilted her head to the side in confusion as she asked that question.

"That's why I'll turn the entire area around us into scorched earth. I'm killing off nature itself, after all," Zagan nodded as his choice was obvious.

"Th-Think it over, Zagan! This is Norden, a holy land that even the church is afraid of setting foot in! Wouldn't it be blasphemy to turn it into scorched earth?" Chastille, who was still in work mode, turned completely pale upon realizing his intentions.

"We're breaking through a barrier born of mysticism, which is drawn from your dear god, so isn't it obvious that it's something blasphemous?"

"Gaaaaaah! Sorcerers really are villains!" Chastille began to thrash about in tears as she said that.

"Dammit, what a pain in the ass! If you're gonna do it, then get it done quick!" Barbatos shouted as he pinned Chastille's arms behind her back to calm her down.

"Will do," Zagan said as he slowly clenched his fist one finger at a time, and then lifted his hand up toward the heavens.

"Burn to ash — Heaven's Phosphor."

A black magic circle woven of mana took shape in his right hand. It was sorcery that made the mana it indiscriminately sucked up combust, leading the mana... no, the very essence of life itself to burn to ash. That was the power Zagan gave birth to in order to kill demons. If he fired it off twice, even the residual thoughts of the Demon Lord could be destroyed.

"I see. You're using the power that destroyed the Sludge Demon Lord, huh? If it's that, then even the elven barrier stands no chance," Gremory said, grinning broadly upon witnessing his display.

Zagan drove his fist into the ground, which made a dull tremor that was followed by bursting black flames. And, after it spread out as if to engulf the earth, it fizzled out. However, everything touched

by the flames turned black and crumbled to ash. The flames even swallowed the elder's manor and reduced it to rubbish… Or well, they should have.

"My goodness… A man who knows naught of holding back, I see."

A hoarse woman's voice rang out from above. Looking up, they spotted a robed shadow above the elder's manor.

The Sigil of the Archdemon on Zagan's right hand throbbed and pounded.

The Sigil of the Archdemon is resonating… That meant the one before his eyes was undoubtedly an Archdemon.

Nephy clung to Zagan's back with a scared look on her face.

"You asshole… How long have you been up there?" Barbatos asked as he and the others raised their guards. However, Zagan put his hand on Barbatos' shoulder and held him back.

"Well, look who's finally decided to show themselves…"

The robed shadow was floating in the air. Because it was already nighttime, it cast no shadow beneath it, so no one was sure whether she was truly there or not. Even so, that person had been lurking around Zagan and the others the entire time.

"Gremory, there's no mistaking that this is that teacher of yours, right?" Zagan questioned Gremory as he kept his eyes trained on the figure.

"Y-Yeah… Without a doubt," Gremory, who usually acted as she pleased, had a cold sweat running down her cheek as she replied in a trembling voice.

At that point, Zagan focused his attention on the traces of his Heaven's Phosphor that vanished before reaching the manor. *It doesn't seem like it was blocked directly… Was some sort of sorcery used to impede the flow of mana?*

157

For example, it was like they separated that area specifically from the rest. Heaven's Phosphor was only able to burn through everything in one area before it vanished, which made that the perfect counter. It seemed like she had thoroughly investigated his abilities and prepared for this confrontation in advance.

That must mean she was watching Bifrons' evening ball... Zagan had only used Heaven's Phosphor on two occasions in the past. Once when he fought the demon chimera, then again at Bifrons' evening ball. At the evening ball, he'd fired it off multiple times to finish off the Sludge Demon Lord. There were a few survivors who did not enlist themselves as Zagan's subordinates, so that was the most likely point where it leaked from.

In any case, Zagan was now convinced that this opponent couldn't be torn apart by Heaven's Phosphor. And based on that conclusion, he began speaking.

"It's been a long time... You're Archdemon Orias, I assume?"

And in response, the robed shadow returned an exaggerated nod before speaking.

"Indeed. I am Orias, Archdemon Zagan."

The robed shadow... Orias, quietly answered him. Zagan then addressed Orias as if speaking to a close friend.

"Sorry, but I'd like to blow that place to smithereens. Could you step aside?"

"My goodness... You certainly obtained power at a terrifying rate, didn't you? The power of a tyrant is quite terrifying," Orias looked down at the burned region of land with pity as she said that, completely ignoring Zagan's question. It seemed Orias had no intention of stepping aside. And so, Zagan knit his brows with a 'Hmm.'

"Were you opposed to me inheriting the title?"

"I didn't oppose it, but I warned that it would be dangerous. Although, nobody even bothered to lend me an ear. I suppose that's only natural, since Archdemons are fundamentally selfish at heart."

In short, unlike Bifrons, Orias was clearly aware that Zagan represented a risk factor. It was only ordinary to eliminate such factors.

It seemed like two Archdemons would clash upon this land, a fact that did not escape Zagan's companions. Every single one of them had sweat pouring down their brows from the strained atmosphere. If a common sorcerer were present, they would surely have fainted from the tense atmosphere alone.

"Will you answer one question?" Zagan asked as he carefully chose his next words.

"Do you think I have any such obligation?"

Zagan choked on the air. Those words must have been woven with mana. And, as if spurred on by his struggle, cracks ran down the stone walls of the house and the sound of lightning striking rang.

Zagan could tell that several of the people behind him couldn't endure it and fell to their knees. Bifrons was an Archdemon who carried a vague sense of eeriness, but Orias was more direct and merciless. And standing before her made Zagan take a step forward with a provocative smile on his face.

"No, I'll have you answer me. Even if you say that you don't want to, I'll drag you down from there and force it out of your lips."

In complete disagreement, Zagan gathered mana and struck it right back at Orias. A vortex of power broke out between the two Archdemons, which made even the trees that were rooted in the earth float up into the air.

"W-Wait, Zagan! This one's too dangerous! I'll… fight too!" Chastille exclaimed despite her pale, clearly frightened face.

Taking a glance back at her, Zagan noticed her hand was trembling as it grasped the hilt of her sheathed sword.

"Don't panic. We're simply talking here. Don't draw your blade, just know that this one isn't some damn brute who is unable to converse," Zagan replied to Chastille in a casual tone.

"A cheap provocation. But, very well. Try asking what you will. I won't necessarily answer, though," Orias squinted as she responded to Zagan.

A snap rang out as the stones and trees floating in the air tore apart. Their fragments grazed Zagan's cheek and drew a faint line of blood. Even as that happened, Zagan smiled like he was enjoying it, and pointed his finger behind him... at Gremory, who was on her knees gasping.

"That nonsensical crap called 'love power' or whatever that Gremory talked about... Tell me, did that come from you?"

Gremory had arbitrarily followed along on what was supposed to be a family trip, toyed around with Nephteros while rambling about love power, and turned into a small girl to trouble Zagan all she wanted. He was curious why she went so far.

"Huh...?" Orias let out an idiotic voice as the overpowering presence that had been dominating the area vanished.

Gremory put her hands on the back of her head and just whistled lightly, her face still drenched in cold sweat.

"Umm... It seems my disciple has been troubling you. Sorry," Orias apologized with a slight bow of her head after stiffening up for a moment.

An apology!? Zagan never expected an Archdemon to lower their head, so he was at a loss for words.

"Miss Gremory, no matter how you put it, embarrassing your esteemed teacher in such a place really is a little…" Kimaris muttered those words, utterly destroying any sense of tension.

"Guuuh, aaagh, Zagan! You don't have to tell her everything!"

"Shut your mouth," Orias cut in.

"Eeek…" Gremory quieted down immediately upon getting scolded by her teacher. Well, Zagan also didn't expect it to be such a serious matter and felt somewhat sorry about it. He fully expected Orias to say, 'Are you making fun of me?' while rushing in to attack…

"I truly am sorry."

"…No, it's fine as long as you understand."

Zagan could do nothing other than awkwardly shake his head in return. And then, Orias spoke as if to revitalize herself.

"I will make up for my disciple's actions at a later date. Sorry, but I cannot allow you to leave this place. Can you not just stay here and live quietly?"

In response to the old woman, who spoke as if rebuking a rowdy pupil, Zagan smiled like he'd heard a good joke.

"I refuse."

"How unfortunate. I didn't really want to turn this place into a battlefield…" Orias said, letting out a deep sigh. And that sigh signaled the start of their battle.

"[Thou art the one who shines like the stars. The one who embraces balance, and arbitrates over good and evil,]" Orias hummed that spell, which made Nephteros turn pale.

"No way… That's my…"

Asteri Ekrexis... It was the celestial mysticism that Nephteros tried to use before. It was also a power that was only supposed to be usable by Nephy and Nephteros, the two high elves. And while gazing at the lights, which floated about the Archdemon like fireflies, Zagan spoke like the situation was no big deal.

"Even if atavism among high elves only happens once every hundred years, both elves and sorcerers possess perpetual youth. It isn't all that strange for a high elf to be several hundred years old."

"Now's not the time for that! If we eat that, there won't even be ashes left, dammit!" Barbatos shouted as he unleashed fire sorcery. No, rather than fire, it was a ray of heat. The stones that were touched by the incandescent band melted as if they were made of mud, and the fallen trees were burned to a crisp in an instant. This person was still one of the very few who were made Archdemon candidates at one point, and it could even be said that his power exceeded Zagan's back when they shared that position. His sorcery was a strike that was comparable to a dragon's breath, but... the moment it touched the light of celestial mysticism, the ray of heat was erased.

"You're... kidding, right?" Barbatos muttered in shock, and Zagan shook his head in response.

"Give it up. Even that Sludge Demon Lord couldn't do anything in the face of that power. It's probably impossible for common sorcery to break through it."

"Common sorcery... That was one of my trump cards!" Barbatos screamed. It was powerful sorcery, but utterly common all the same. Unless it was sorcery that focused solely on offense that was as powerful as celestial mysticism or Zagan's sorcery, it would be impossible to pierce Orias' defenses. And unfortunately, that meant an ordinary sorcerer possessed no means of attacking Orias.

"[Be that as it may, balance is broken. Order is lost, and the earth is dyed in blood. Thus, this merits retribution. By the hammer that pardons all sin,]" Orias moved to the next verse of the spell as their conversation transpired. The lights that were protecting her changed directions and rained down on Zagan and the others.

"You lot, stay behind me," Zagan held up his arm as he barked orders at his companions. And then, a single shining magic circle floated up atop it.

"Heaven's Scale? But how will a single one of those do anything..."

As the counterpart sorcery to Heaven's Phosphor, it earnestly absorbed mana from its surroundings and continued to amplify in intensity. Given enough time, it could become a shield that could withstand a single strike from celestial mysticism, but regrettably, its size was only about large enough to fit in one's palm.

Since the lights created by Orias easily surpassed a hundred, Zagan's shield was far too flimsy to protect himself, let alone the rest of his companions. But even so, Zagan showed no sign of panicking and simply shook his head.

"Well, just watch," Zagan said as he used the small magic circle to repel the falling lights one by one. However, it was just a vain struggle in the end. The lights spread out as if to envelop Zagan. And as they did, Orias continued chanting the spell, heading into the last verse of her celestial mysticism in a booming voice.

"[The lights of the heavens are all stars. All that shines far and wide plummets into a conflagration. With no compassion, no grief, it simply judges and brings destruction. This is the prayer of atonement] — Asteri Ekrexis!"

The lights descending upon Zagan converged on a single point and then exploded. And immediately following that, an intense light shot out as if to pierce the heavens.

The celestial mysticism Nephy used solemnly erased everything, but Orias' induced a violent explosion instead.

"Hmm... So this is the completed form of the celestial mysticism you tried to use last time, huh? What a good opportunity. Study it to your heart's content, Nephteros," Zagan muttered with great interest as he stared at the vivid light. He spoke casually as the light settled down without even leaving a single scratch, or even a speck of soot, on them...

"This is... the sorcery that struck Master Bifrons?" Nephteros gulped audibly as she took in the sight. A simplified version of this sorcery was planted in the stationary that Nephteros carried. Just as she said, it possessed enough power to strike even an Archdemon dead.

"Ridiculous... It's a... dragon?" Orias opened her eyes wide as she said that. She saw that an enormous dragon was protecting Zagan and the others. Though, having said that, it wasn't a living, breathing dragon, but one made of light woven with mana.

"So pretty... It looks like Father," Foll let out a voice filled with amazement from Kimaris' back.

"Heaven's Scale — Dragon Form... Just think of it as a golem formed by Heaven's Scale," Zagan said, petting Foll's head all the while. The mana that composed the dragon's body was drawn in by Heaven's Scale, which meant even celestial mysticism wasn't enough to break through this armor. However, even more impressive than its intensity was the fact that it absorbed both mana and aura and made use of them to enhance itself. That meant all attacks which used either of those as a source would be weakened. Be it sorcery or

Sacred Swords, they would be unable to draw out even half of their original power as long as it stayed up.

"Is this… a dragon's magic formula?" Barbatos asked as he let out a groan.

"Yeah. Foll taught it to me," Zagan replied. It wasn't like Zagan kept Foll by his side just because she was cute. Even if she was still a child, there was much knowledge to be learned from one of the few living dragons. That was why Foll was Zagan's beloved daughter, his colleague in learning sorcery, and also his teacher.

"Heaven's Scale was originally sorcery based on a dragon's scale, after all. This form is only a natural evolution," Zagan claimed as he stroked the neck of the dragon golem. He wasn't simply content with making sorcery that was just solid. Using this form as a base, he created Heaven's Scale to reinforce his theory. Looking up at the dragon, which splendidly withstood Asteri Ekrexis, Zagan nodded in satisfaction.

Celestial mysticism really is powerful, but having said that, it isn't like it surpasses sorcery entirely… In the end, it simply had a different structure. If used properly by skilled individuals, either could be the strongest. Zagan was unable to use celestial mysticism, but he was able to create sorcery capable of withstanding it.

"Well, it probably doesn't actually compare with Wise Dragon Orobas, but there are dragons with this form too," Zagan claimed. He didn't know how it looked to Foll, who actually knew the real Orobas, but this was the form of a powerful dragon in Zagan's mind.

"Daddy, so cool…" Foll's amber eyes sparkled, and for some reason, she then took a deep breath as she said that. It seemed Foll thought this was an appropriate moment to call Zagan that.

"…Mm!" Zagan felt ready to fall to his knees as he desperately clutched his chest to withstand her assault. Then, he returned a smile to her and looked over to Orias.

"I'll say it one more time… I want to blow that place away. Do you mind stepping aside?"

"…I see. Even I can't put up much of a fight, huh?" Orias' face twisted in displeasure as she made that fact known. The act of brushing off the sparks that happened to fall about you couldn't be called a fight. That was why Zagan had no intention of fighting. Just as he declared, he wanted to blow away the elder's manor and was just waiting for Orias to get out of the way. If it was a fight, Zagan would not ease his attacks at all until he choked the life out of his opponent.

But, I guess I waited long enough, huh? Zagan pointed at the manor with a snap. And then, the dragon's head turned toward it in response.

"I'm the type who always follows through on their word. I won't give you a third warning," Zagan proclaimed. And following that, he spoke a single word as if passing judgment, "Fire!"

"Erk…" Orias opened her eyes wide and leaped off the roof as the dragon shot its breath at the manor. Immediately following that, the building was pierced by the light and disintegrated. Since she was protecting it, it was likely Orias had formed defenses around it, but the breath of light washed over everything easily. And at the same time, the dragon golem's body dispersed and vanished.

Heaven's Scale was sorcery that increased its strength by absorbing the power around it. Woven into the form of a large dragon, it ate all the surrounding mana and aura, including the celestial mysticism, to swell in power and transform into a breath attack.

Before long, after the light settled down, all that was left was the vitrified ground stretching out where the manor once stood.

Mm. How refreshing... It was the house of the elf who hurt Nephy. Honestly speaking, he felt it would be fine to revive them as undead and torment them some more, but Nephy did not wish for such a thing. That was why he decided to settle with just annihilating the proof of their existence.

"Hmm... Well, that's about all it can do, I suppose."

"That's... about all, you say? Are you saying that destructive force is still lacking in some way?" Nephteros muttered while trembling.

Zagan pointed in the direction the breath was fired. Off in the distance, illuminated by the moonlight, was glassed earth that stopped after a point. And once they looked beyond that, they could see the same peaceful forest as before.

"The boundary of the barrier is probably somewhere around there. The dragon golem is unable to destroy this barrier. I have no objection to its defensive strength, but its destructive power is still lacking, yes."

"How terrifying..." Nephteros muttered as a line of sweat ran down her cheek.

Eventually, Zagan looked over to Orias, who managed to escape the breath. It was unlikely that she got away unscathed at such a short range, but even now, Orias refused to remove her hood.

"Sorry for making a racket. We'll be leaving now, so why don't you undo the barrier around here?" Zagan asked.

"I believe I already told you that I cannot allow all of you to leave this place," Orias solemnly stated.

"Well, you can insist on anything that you want, but is that alright?" Zagan asked for confirmation as if he was showing her mercy, which left Orias staring back at him in wonder.

"...What?"

"Whether or not you undo the barrier, we'll be leaving this place. Are you sure it's fine to keep opposing us?" Zagan inquired. He'd displayed a shield thus far, which meant he hadn't even begun attacking. There was no way his fellow Archdemon hadn't clued in to that fact.

"Don't make me repeat myself," Orias said as she audibly gulped, refusing to step aside. Then, she placed her hands on the ground and began muttering something.

Celestial mysticism again...? No, it doesn't seem like it... The sigil on Zagan's right hand began to heat up. It seemed she was using the Sigil of the Archdemon to do something.

I have a means of sealing it before it happens, but... Zagan had the option to use resonance to render the sigil powerless. However, he also felt like making use of the chance to witness another Archdemon getting serious. And so, he folded his arms and decided to wait for what Orias was doing to finish. And upon seeing that, Barbatos yelled out in shock.

"Oh, come on! We're in deep shit here, Zagan! Kill that bastard already!"

Ignoring him, Zagan kept waiting, which eventually made him notice that he recognized the magic circle that spread out beneath Orias' feet.

"I see... The magic circle for summoning demons, huh?"

Barbatos had used the entire entrance hall of a castle to create the magic circle, and it took him many months, yet Orias had managed it in the space between her two hands with no preparation.

Back when he first came face to face with a real demon, Zagan's only option was to use the Sigil of the Archdemon to send it back. If he tried to fight it at the time, he would have perished. And that demon was once more appearing before Zagan. Miasma blew out of the magic circle, and the complexion of all the other sorcerers present changed.

"I'm joining in, Sir Zagan!" Kimaris let out a howl as the atmosphere warped.

"Tch, don't resent me for this, teacher!"

"I'll help."

Gremory unleashed her evil eye and Foll matched it with her dragon's breath. The three of them unleashed the powers unique to their races and wove sorcery into them as an attack. Each and every one of them possessed destructive power that made Barbatos' heat ray look like mere child's play. However, the three of them all turned pale. Before those attacks reached Orias, they all vanished, seemingly obstructed by an invisible wall.

"The miasma… became a bulwark!?"

Even the three of them combined were unable to pierce through the thick wall of miasma.

"Then, if it's celestial mysticism—" Nephteros stretched out her hands to assist. And, as she chanted out a spell in Celestian, several crystal stakes shot out of the ground. They certainly did pierce through the wall of miasma, but…

"Th-They stopped?"

Right before the crystal stakes reached Orias, they came to a halt. Sweat ran down Nephteros' brow, and a helpless sense of panic crept across her face.

"It's no good… Ugh… The hegemony of my mysticism… is being snatched away… Agh!" Nephteros was clearly resisting, but

the crystals wouldn't budge an inch. In the next instant, the crystals changed directions and rained down on Zagan's group.

"Shine — Sacred Sword Azrael!" Chastille forced her way to the front and brought forth the Light of Purification from her Sacred Sword. This was the first time Zagan witnessed her drawing out her full power with both her Anointed Armor and Sacred Sword equipped.

"HYAAA!" Chastille roared, unleashing over ten slashes to smash the crystal stakes to pieces.

Hm... So when she's decked out, she can even destroy celestial mysticism, huh? Zagan admired her strength, but Chastille's expression remained stern.

"Ugh, the wall is already repairing itself..." Chastille complained.

Upon closer inspection, it was clear that the holes Nephteros made in the wall of miasma were repairing themselves to protect Orias. As things stood, even if Chastille cut into it, she would never reach the Archdemon.

"Hm... I guess nothing can be done, then," Zagan claimed in a tone of surrender. An Archdemon was right before them, brazenly weaving together a magic circle, which was rather fitting for someone of her stature. After all, there was no way someone of their power would just expose themselves.

"Can't you break through that, Zagan?" Chastille glared back at him sternly, clearly not believing his words.

"No, it's useless. That's not sorcery, so I can't devour it. Plus, the dragon golem is defensive sorcery, so it's only able to display that destructive force after it's attacked."

The dragon golem was, effectively, a barrier of sorts. It couldn't launch an attack on its own.

"What about Heaven's Phosphor?"

"Did you forget that she just defended against it? Do you think an Archdemon is dumb enough to get hit by sorcery they've already avoided before?"

In short, Zagan possessed no means of stopping Orias from summoning a demon. *Well, there's a need to keep her alive, after all. If it was fine to kill her, then I have options, but…*

"Well, it's a good opportunity. I'll have you show me the power of a demon," Zagan said, shrugging his shoulders as he spoke.

"…P-Please cut the jokes. Did you forget? That is not something human hands can deal with. Even Wise Dragon Orobas had to trade his life to defeat one!"

Hearing Orobas' name made Foll tremble.

"You're right. It's an enemy that even a legendary dragon couldn't overpower. If we can get away without having to fight it, then we should do so," Zagan said as he aimed a nod at Chastille.

"Then—"

"However, when one eventually appears before your eyes, what do you plan to do?"

"Ugh…"

A demon had already appeared in this world. Orobas and Raphael fought against it and lost something far too great in the process. Given their strength, if the demons ever appeared as a group, then the world would surely be in peril, and this girl would have to face them head-on.

"That's why… I think this is a chance for us to learn about demons. You aren't a sorcerer, but you still shouldn't waste a research opportunity like this," Zagan said as he placed his hand on Chastille's head with a thud. Then, he looked over to Orias and watched a dark mana accompanied by a grotesque 'something' crawl out of the magic circle. Chastille tried to step to the front with her

171

Sacred Sword at the ready, but her hands were shaking. The other sorcerers were reacting much the same. Even Nephteros couldn't get her voice out.

Before long, a strange figure appeared. It had a flimsy body that was thin as paper, and though it had a head, it seemed to have no face. Its limbs took on the form of some sort of twisted pinwheel unlike any type of living creature. And above all else, it was big. Orias was riding on its shoulder, high up enough to look down on the area's treeline.

"H-Hey, compared to the one last time, this is…" Barbatos gasped and opened his mouth to speak.

"Yeah, you're right," Zagan said as he nodded in agreement.

This one is far more powerful than the demon Barbatos' magic circle summoned… Perhaps it was because of the power of the Sigil of the Archdemon, but all anybody could do in the face of such a thing was turn pale and open their mouths in shock.

"Don't think you can stop this with the Sigil of the Archdemon. If you are unable to defeat this, your future will be forfeit," Orias claimed as she let out a laugh. She also possessed a sigil, so even if Zagan somehow made her lose control of the demon, she could simply regain it. However, that didn't mean he wouldn't fight.

"Since it's a demon, it's fine to kill it, I guess…" Zagan said, itching to pick a fight.

The demon began to move. And just as Zagan thought it was about to swing what it had for an arm with a flutter, a countless number of stakes jutted out of its body.

"Th-The hell!?" Barbatos yelled upon seeing such an unpredictable attack from its somewhat human-shaped body, but by that time, Zagan already had his left hand up.

"Heaven's Scale — Dragon Form."

He wove the dragon of light in an instant, and its body stood to protect Zagan's group. The demon's stakes were obstructed by the scales of light, and not even a single one was able to reach Zagan.

For the time being, it looks like even a demon's attack can be mitigated... That was a pleasant discovery, as it meant even the demons used the same source of power as humans.

"With that power, even if you can stop a demon, you'll never be able to defeat it!" Orias roared out at him. It almost sounded like Orias was telling him to show her that he could defeat it.

"That goes without saying," Zagan said as he raised his right hand. He didn't clench his fist, choosing to stick out his fingers as if scratching the air instead. Mana converged at his fingertips and wove a magic circle. And upon seeing that, Gremory and Kimaris' faces stiffened.

"Erk... Everyone get back!"

"Lady Foll, Lady Nephy, please hold fast to my mane!"

Gremory grabbed Nephteros from behind and leaped back while carrying her, and Kimaris placed Nephy and Foll under his arms as he distanced himself from Zagan.

"Hey, Crybaby, this looks bad. Get outta there."

"Don't call me a crybaby!" Chastille yelled. Though she surely sensed the danger as well, since she leaped back with her Sacred Sword still at the ready.

After confirming that everybody had escaped his effective range, Zagan swung his right hand down.

"Heaven's Phosphor — Fivefold Grand Flower."

Five black strands ran down from Zagan's fingers. They resembled both outstanding blades and a cluster of amaryllis. The five blades fired out in all directions, cutting through the demon's stakes and piercing into its body.

173

"…Wh-Wh-Whoa!" Orias stammered.

Following that, a black flower bloomed. The upper body of the demon, which had been pierced by five blades, ruptured. The entity that Zagan could once do naught but cower against was annihilated by a single strike.

"Ridiculous… What did you do?" Orias muttered as she fell to the ground.

"It's nothing impressive, really. All I did was drive five Heaven Phosphors into it at once."

Unlike the fire that spread out indiscriminately, the blade form was condensed and gave Heaven's Phosphor a focused area of effect. And he used it five times. That was not as simple as he made it sound.

When I fought the Sludge Demon Lord, all it could reach was its outer surface, but this is different… Back then, if he could have just reached its core, then they wouldn't have been pushed into such a tough spot. In order to make up for that, he went on to pile improvements onto the spell, and what he arrived at was the Fivefold Grand Flower.

Gremory and Kimaris both witnessed its trial run. And thanks to that, they knew getting caught in it would result in their deaths. After all, since it was a spell that burned its target from the inside out, anything struck by it would eventually burst. The way it did so was akin to a blooming flower, hence Fivefold Grand Flower.

"Whoops, looks like there was too much power and it ended up breaking the barrier…"

The remnants of what finished off the demon even seemed to bring down the village's barrier. Orias sank to the floor and drooped her shoulders. As one would expect, she didn't seem to have any more hands to play. All she did was bite down on her lips, unable to

even speak. In other words, even a mighty Archdemon was unable to compete with Zagan.

"Just kill me. You won… and I lost."

"Indeed. That is surely the proper way to go about things, but I still have one piece of business with you."

"Business… you say?"

"Well, it isn't that big a deal, but…" Zagan removed Orias' hood, then continued, "You're not really Orias, are you, Titania?"

The face under the hood was that of an old woman, but she very clearly resembled Nephy.

"She's… Titania? Wait, wasn't she killed by Orias?"

As the battle came to an end, Barbatos and the others came back towards Zagan, and they couldn't believe what he was saying.

"You didn't get struck down by Orias. You defeated him and took his Sigil of the Archdemon, right?"

Of course, the Archdemons who personally knew the real Orias would have realized that fact, but most sorcerers had little interest in the affairs of others. The other Archdemons surely took no notice of an Archdemon who was defeated by a lesser sorcerer.

"Then why didn't she create an elf country or whatever? Wasn't that why she picked a fight with an Archdemon?" Barbatos voiced his doubts.

"She probably lost the chance to do so. No, it's more accurate to say the meaning of creating one was lost, right?"

Titania may have defeated Orias, but it cost her everything she had. Her comrades, her reason for living, and everything else. That was what it meant to make an enemy of an Archdemon.

She probably took Gremory in as a disciple because they're both part of a dying race... Fomorians were almost as rare as elves. If one were to search the entire continent, they wouldn't even find a hundred of them. Zagan assumed some sort of sympathy may have welled up in Orias due to her loneliness.

"Everything from here is just my conjecture, but you were probably born in this village. I don't know how you were treated here, but after fighting Orias, you decided that it was still better here than the outside world. That was why you came to entrust Nephy to them. Am I wrong?"

"..." Orias didn't answer, but her silence made her response evident.

"But, in that case, why did she turn Nephy into a child? Also, why did she seal us in here?" Chastille asked as she tilted her head to the side.

"You don't get it?" Zagan made an exasperated expression as he replied.

"Oh, come on! Don't be so mean!?" Chastille whined. It seemed her crybaby persona had returned now that their conflict had been resolved.

"Nephy is this woman's daughter..." Zagan proclaimed.

That line made Orias let out a sigh of resignation.

"My goodness. This is the first time I've felt that bluffing is pointless," Orias said as she looked over to Nephy. Then, she continued with, "Little Lady, do you enjoy your life with these people here?"

"Yes. Mashter Zagan, Big Shish Foll, and everybody else are very kind to me."

This was surely a difficult conversation for Nephy to follow in her current form, as she couldn't have known her relationship with the old lady before her.

Actually, she may be taking on the form of an old woman to hide that fact... The portrait in the pendant showed a young woman, and as Gremory's teacher, she likely had the ability to manipulate her age at will.

"Okay, that's good. You see, Granny here thought it would be wonderful to make such fun times go on forever," Orias responded with a gentle nod.

"That... makes me very happy, but it's no good. Mashter Zagan has a lot of work. Also, I want to quickly get bigger and help him..." Nephy said with a troubled expression on her face.

"I was sure that would be the case, but I wanted to force those fun times on you regardless of your opinion," Orias claimed as she beckoned Nephy over, then said, "Come now, over here. It's about time to go home, right? I'll remove the princess' curse."

As Orias touched her forehead, Nephy gently collapsed on the spot. And then, Orias placed a robe on her shoulders.

"She'll return to her original form in about thirty minutes or so," Orias stated, staring at Zagan. Then, she said, "It's just as you say. I defeated Orias, but I lost everything in the process. Even though I left this village because I wanted to create a paradise for those who were oppressed, everyone died because of me."

Nobody in the world could understand the despair she felt at that time.

"Orias was a convenient name that let me toss aside my connection to the elves. After that, well, you can imagine whatever you will," Orias claimed as she held up the Sigil of the Archdemon

on her right hand. Then, with a tired sigh, she said, "So, did you keep this decrepit old woman alive just to speak of such nonsense?"

"Not at all. Well, hearing your old stories isn't all that bad, either…"

Yes. The real issue at hand was still to come. Zagan stood before Orias. And as he raised his right hand, which was strong enough to slaughter even a demon, Chastille and the others turned pale.

"H-Hold on, Zagan! Isn't that person, um… Nephy's mother? Killing her would mean…" Chastille began wailing about something, but Zagan paid her no mind and swung his arm down.

"Urk…" Orias' body stiffened up, but the next instant, her face was steeped in bewilderment. Zagan put his hand to his chest and knelt down before Orias.

"Titania. I'm in love with your daughter. Please give Nephy to me."

"Huh, um, huh…?" Orias — no, Titania's mouth opened with a pop. She let out a bewildered sound that was unfitting of an Archdemon, but eventually, she muttered as if she couldn't believe it. This was the real reason that Zagan didn't fight her. Ultimately, the only thing Zagan attacked was the demon. He did not inflict a single wound on Orias herself.

The only one allowed to kill Nephy's blood is Nephy herself… Well, killing her own relatives was a problem in itself, but unfortunately, Zagan didn't possess such upright sensibilities.

The main problem was whether Zagan possessed enough power to force an Archdemon to capitulate without actually fighting, but that ended up being not too difficult.

"Give you my daughter, you say…? Do you mean you want to take Nephy as your wife…?" Orias replied in a doubtful tone.

"That's right."

"Is that... something that you need my permission for?"

"You're alive, and you wish for Nephy's happiness. Do I need another reason?" Zagan asked. He didn't understand the concept of parent-child relationships very well. However, if Foll were to find a lover one day, then Zagan himself would never permit it unless he approved of them. And in that case, he thought he should pay respects to Nephy's parent.

"That child... already belongs to you, doesn't she? Still, allow me to say this..." Orias said with a laugh. And then, she bowed her head.

"Please take care of my daughter."

And with that, the curtain came down on Nephy's visit home.

"Now then, I'll be taking my leave before Nephelia wakes up."

"Oh, hold on, wait a sec," Zagan made Orias stop as she put on her hood and turned to walk away.

"...Do you still need something?" Orias inquired with a puzzled expression on her face.

"You were just defeated by another Archdemon. Do you think you can just walk away?" Zagan responded in astonishment.

Hearing such words, which completely put all the sincerity just moments before to waste, made everyone stiffen up.

"Z-Zagan, she's Nephy's mother. Treating her any more poorly is..."

"I'm not really one to talk, but my teacher isn't really a villain here, you know? She may be an odd one, but she would never cause you any harm, or how should I put it..."

In an unusual turn, both Chastille and Gremory were in agreement as they tried to stop him. However, Zagan silenced them with a single glare.

"Sanctions are placed on the defeated. There are no exceptions, regardless of if they are an Archdemon or anybody's parent."

In order to protect Nephy and Foll, Zagan had to continue demonstrating that it was a bad idea to make an enemy of him. Barbatos, Raphael, and even Archdemon Bifrons, didn't get away without some form of punishment... Bifrons had even died several

181

times over already. That was why Zagan couldn't yield this point. Not everyone would believe that what Zagan was doing was correct. However, even if it was wrong, they were unable to refute his point. No one called out to stop him at that point.

The only one who reacted was Barbatos, who snorted as if he was watching some sort of farce. And so, Zagan decided to slug him in the face later.

"It's obvious reasoning for a sorcerer, isn't it? Well, I'm also getting tired of this long life. If you're willing to ensure Nephelia's safety, then I have no objections," Orias showed no signs of resisting and stood before Zagan as she said that.

"How gracious. Then, I'll have you take your punishment," Zagan declared. Then, he looked over to Barbatos and said, "Hey, Barbatos. Hand that over."

"...You really got some nerve, huh?" Barbatos seemed to get what he was saying and stuck his hand into a shadow as he responded. And what he pulled out... was a single bottle of liquor. Taking the bottle, Zagan spoke to Orias once more.

"You come from this village, right? The liquor here isn't all that bad... but that fit of rage just blew up the brewery."

"And what about it?" Orias asked, knitting her brows like she couldn't tell what Zagan was getting at.

"Obtain more of this liquor and bring it as a tribute to my castle. That's your punishment."

"You want me... to go to your castle?" Orias repeated his demand as if searching for his true intentions, and her gaze naturally wandered over to Nephy.

"It can't be... Are you telling me to meet with Nephelia?"

"Who knows. Though, even if you somehow coincidentally meet Nephy at my castle, I'd have no complaints."

"…And how much time do I get to accomplish that task?" Orias probed, a bitter smile on her face.

"I don't have that much spare time, so I don't plan on waiting very long."

"How strict."

"It's your punishment, after all."

"The vanquished shall obey the victor. Such is the providence of the world," Orias stated as she bowed her head in an exaggerated manner.

He didn't know just how long it would take Orias to put her feelings in order after having abandoned her daughter once already. Plus, even if Nephy were to reunite with her, it could end in tragedy.

Even so, if she prayed for Nephy's happiness, then she has the right to meet her… That was why Zagan provided her with the opportunity to do so.

"…I never thought the day would come where my courage would be tested," Orias' figure vanished like a shadow as she left those parting words behind. And after her presence completely vanished, Barbatos spoke up in an exasperated tone.

"You really never fucking change, huh?"

"Shut it. Why don't you think of another way of doing it?"

"Ain't it fine to kill them?"

"In that case, I'll start by killing you," Zagan replied with a glare on his face.

"Heehee, I have no intentions of displeasing you, Master," Barbatos said as he let out a mocking laugh.

"Barbatos, you knew? That Zagan would do this, I mean…" Chastille asked with a look of shock on her face.

"I mean, why do you even think I'm still alive?" Barbatos was also left to live on the condition that he brought over liquor as a

tribute. He wasn't stupid enough to not realize what was going on when things were going along the exact same lines. However, the only one making a surprised expression here was Chastille.

"You're so dumb, Horse Head. How did you not realize when you've known Zagan longer than me?" Foll spoke while stifling a yawn.

"Huh?"

Foll had also listened to the farce just now partway through while relaxing on Kimaris' back. Well, seeing as it was evening and normally the time for her to be in bed, that made perfect sense.

"Th-Then, what about you, Kimaris? You didn't know, right?"

"No, considering Sir Zagan's personality, I thought it would be a little far fetched for him to kill Miss Orias," Kimaris stated as he looked back at Chastille with a disappointed expression on his face. Chastille was gradually being reduced to tears. And then, she called out to Gremory as if clinging on to her last hope.

"Ugh, Gremory, you say something too! Weren't you also panicking!?"

In an unusual turn, Gremory's cheeks reddened as she covered her face in response to that question.

So even she still possesses the general notion of shame, huh...? It was somehow relieving, and Gremory then spoke in a tearful voice.

"J-Just forget about it. I just lost my composure because it concerned my teacher. If I end up having the same reaction as this one over and over... then... I... I'd just have to die."

"Is that really something worth dying over!?" Chastille yelped, bursting into tears at that point.

Ah, looks like office hours are over... The gallant Archangel was certainly reliable, but in the end, Zagan couldn't really relax if she

didn't act like her usual self. And thanks to her crying, Nephy began stirring in Zagan's arms.

"Hm... Hm...?"

"Nephy!" Zagan called out to her, which made everyone else gather around.

"Master Zagan... Huh...? Um, what... happened to me...?" Nephy was only able to let out a bewildered voice because her memories were a mess.

"Nephy, do you not remember what happened?" Zagan asked, but Nephy's ears simply quivered in confusion. Watching her reaction, he got a real sense that Nephy was back to normal. She cast her gaze down as if searching through her memories, and then was taken aback.

"That's right, Master Zagan! A sorcerer is lurking about here. Judging by their power... they're likely an Archdemon..."

With that, Zagan felt relieved, yet somehow disappointed.

She doesn't remember the time when she was small, I guess... The young girl who could laugh innocently and tell him she loved him was gone. Was this truly alright? Such doubts floated up in Zagan's mind, but he shook his head as if to rid himself of all those thoughts.

"That one wasn't an enemy, so you don't need to worry anymore," Zagan claimed as he brushed Nephy's head.

It was just a dream in her mind. However, Nephy blinked in surprise when she looked over to Zagan's chest. There, she caught a glimpse of the wreath he received from the little Nephy.

"This... is what I made together with Big Sis Foll..." Nephy stated as she stretched her hand timidly out to the wreath. It seemed there were portions she vaguely remembered.

"Master Zagan, did we.. talk about something very important?" Nephy asked, looking rather taken aback.

"Something very important…? No, I don't think so.." Zagan tilted his head to the side as he replied, but Nephy shook her head as her white hair swayed around.

"No, there must have been something. If I remember right, we were in front of a fireplace, and you said something…"

"Huh?"

In front of a fireplace… Something very important… Those words made Zagan remember what transpired earlier.

"Nephy, I love you. That's why I'll take back the Nephy that I love." That was the moment Zagan, who could never say the words 'I love you,' first relayed his feelings to Nephy. And as Zagan began panicking, the first one to move was Kimaris.

"Miss Gremory, shall we talk over there?"

"Let me go, Kimaris! Don't make me miss out on a once in a lifetime display of love power! I'm telling you to let me gooooooooooooooooooo!"

Kimaris pulled Gremory away as she wailed in an unsightly manner. Next, Chastille blocked Foll's vision with both her hands.

"Horse Head. I can't see."

"Sorry, but it's too soon for you to watch. Lord Raphael would surely do the same," Chastille declared, seemingly blocking Foll's vision in place of the butler who was waiting back at the castle. And just like that, she took Foll away, as well. The last one left, Barbatos, seemed to have no interest at all from the very beginning and was leaning against a tree while knocking back a bottle of liquor.

With all his paths of retreat cut off before he even knew it, Zagan let out a groan.

"Ah, um, Nephy. About that time…"

"Yes?" Nephy's azure eyes looked directly into his as she responded to him.

If I run away here, I feel like I'll never be able to tell her my feelings... It would be far too pitiful for him to run away when he tasked Orias with something so difficult already. And so, Zagan gathered his resolve.

"Nephy."

"Yes?"

"Please wait... about ten seconds."

"...Okay," Nephy nodded, nearly making a bitter smile. If Zagan was able to just tell Nephy that he loved her, he wouldn't have made her wait so long in the first place, so his delay was only natural.

Zagan took a deep breath to calm himself down, but ten seconds was far too short. By the time he took his third breath, time was already up. And then, opening his eyes with a snap, he said...

"Nephy!"

"Y-Yes."

"...I'll only say this once, got it?" Zagan proclaimed as he embraced her. Then, he whispered into her pointy ears.

"I love you, Nephy. I've been in love with you for so, so long..." Zagan stated before quickly realizing he should have said it in a more eloquent manner. However, Nephy simply put her strength into her arms and tightly squeezed Zagan's back.

A sweet scent wafted out. She was soft and slender, but even so, the way she put all her effort into embracing him made Zagan's heart beat like a drum. Plus, Zagan could tell that Nephy's heart was also thudding rapidly.

"Yes. I remember!" Nephy happily replied. And Zagan could tell his face was getting red due to her words.

Dammit, does Nephy actually remember everything? In that case, it would have been better for him not to say anything. However,

looking at the way her ears were happily jumping up and down, he couldn't get angry at her.

Did she just… want to hear it one more time? Regardless of the answer to that question, she knew she was loved now. And so, Nephy brought her mouth close to Zagan's ear and whispered into it.

"I also… love you, Master Zagan. I love you so much. I am really, truly in love with you."

That surprise attack made Zagan rub his cheek against Nephy's. Chastille, on the other hand, was staring at them and blushing all the way to her ears. Gremory was in high spirits, clamoring about something. Barbatos was letting out an ostentatious belch. And Foll was kicking Chastille's shins.

Frankly, all of them were ruining the atmosphere. But still, Zagan felt like forgiving all of it.

Unfortunately, Zagan failed to notice one important fact at that time.

Nephteros was nowhere to be found…

"…Hmm. Did you have some business with me?" Orias inquired.

Inside the dense forest.

Nephteros erased her presence and chased after Orias. Before long, her pursuit was noticed, and Orias stopped walking and called out to her. As Nephteros revealed herself, Orias nodded in understanding.

"You're… I see. You aren't Zagan's subordinate, but Bifrons', correct?" Orias replied with no hint of hostility in her voice. But even so, Nephteros felt ready to fall to her knees as their eyes met.

Zagan managed to defeat this monster so handily...? Everyone else in the village combined were unable to even lay a finger on Orias, but he defeated her all on his own. How terrifying. And an audible gulp made Nephteros' fear resound from within her throat. It made her hate herself for creating a situation where she was meeting with an Archdemon on her own. It wasn't like Nephteros was under Zagan's protection. If she displeased someone who had no reason to keep her alive, then she would surely die.

This was how Archdemons were, and Orias was one of them. Still, Nephteros mustered her willpower and opened her mouth to speak.

"Please, somehow forgive my discourtesy. I have come forth... because there is something that I would like to ask you."

"I'm in a good mood right now. There is no need to humble yourself," Orias said as she shrugged her shoulders.

"I see," Nephteros said, turning pale and pitifully trembling, despite Orias' gentle tone. This Archdemon was certainly scary. However, potentially learning the answer to what she wanted to ask was also quite frightening.

"Go on. Speak. It seems Zagan has taken a liking to you, so I will do you no harm," Orias stated in a comforting tone. Somehow, her words almost seemed to be filled with pity.

"You are... Nephelia's mother, are you not?" Nephteros asked as she finally managed to gather her resolve.

"...I am. Though, if possible, I would prefer you not speak of it."

"My apologies. However, this is an important matter," Nephteros replied with a quick bow. Then, she asked, "Do you... have any other children?"

"Hmm...? I don't really understand the point of your question. What do you mean?"

189

"I... have the same face as Nephelia. I have the same white hair, and am also well-versed in Celestian," Nephteros replied while nervously gulping down all the saliva in her mouth. And then, while touching her own face, she continued, "But I don't have any memories... I remember nothing of my childhood... or my family..."

Above all else, she was scared that she had never even doubted that fact before. Her voice was trembling in an unsightly manner as her face twisted, ready to burst in tears at any moment.

"Just... what am I?"

And in response, Orias said...

To be continued...

Afterword

It's been a long time. I have come to deliver *An Archdemon's Dilemma: How to Love Your Elf Bride Volume 4*. My name is Fuminori Teshima.

The main focus of this volume? 'My bride has turned into a little girl, so how should I show my love for her?' On a visit to Nephy's hometown, Nephy ends up turning into a child. Foll is happy to be a big sister, Gremory runs wild in her child form, and, for some reason, Nephteros gets caught up in the mix! However, among all that, the one who remains most levelheaded is Chastille. Will you turn Nephy back to being your bride, or will you raise her as a daughter!? It's time to choose, Zagan!

Well, that's the gist of this arc.

Perhaps due to Nephy becoming smaller, Nephteros hangs around a fair bit more than usual. It's also quite fresh to have Nephy show so many different expressions in the illustrations.

Also, contrary to my expectations as the author, Gremory, who was kind of a side character in volume 3, has taken center stage. Thanks to that, I feel like the plot ended up diverging a lot, but, well, that's not a really a big deal. Honestly, I'm just really glad that my chief editor, K, didn't put a stop to Nephteros' scene with Gremory.

I mean, I *really* enjoyed that scene.

Wasn't it nice? This is just my personal opinion, but I prefer that kind of relationship to people getting all clingy all the time… It's also

nice when there's a couple with an age gap, right? Like a middle-aged boss and a new recruit. Or wait, maybe more like an experienced butler and a new maid?

You know where one is really noisy and boisterous, but the other is stoic and silent? Or like, a very earnest young girl who's also foul-mouthed and lonely. It's really great when those types of characters start to open their hearts. And by that logic, the pairing of an eccentric granny and a young girl is nice too, isn't it? Like, the granny looks all lonely when the girl isn't there, and then the girl shows up and the granny frowns to hide her embarrassment... Ah, that thought warms my heart...

Hold on, this afterword is getting awfully long, isn't it? Guess I spent too much time talking about how the plot was shaped by my feti— No, um, I've just been speaking about things totally unrelated to this book. Anyway, enough about those hobbies. Though, speaking of hobbies, the compressor for my airbrush broke, so I got a brand new one. Using precise tools makes things a lot more fun, so I'm honestly glad I have a new model. The tablet that I've been using also broke, which means I've got a new one of those, too! And I got a kind that pros use, to boot! What's really amazing is that when I draw a straight line, it doesn't bend at all. Makes drawing a whole lot easier!

I think the next volume will focus on Nephteros, who had an awfully turbulent ending this time around, and Chastille, who's been working herself to death. Since it involves Chastille, maybe a new character from the church will appear? Also, this time around, Zagan and Nephy made their relationship clear, but they have no idea how a normal couple acts. That's got me real fired up to write *An Archdemon's Dilemma: How to Love your Elf Bride Volume 5*. Hopefully, I can release it this spring.

Oh, one more thing! The news is already out, but the manga adaptation of this story is going well. They showed me the key visuals

ahead of time and assured me that they're doing everything they can to keep the tone consistent with my work. I'm looking forward to the complete product.

The serialization date for the manga may not be set by the time you read this afterword, but I hope we'll be able to deliver it to you soon. Please look forward to it!

As for my other plans, this volume was supposed to be a new publication for January, but it ended up getting shuffled around because of the new year's schedule. That's why it's going on sale in December, the same month as the novelization of 'Desktop Army: The Evil Tower of Rapunzel,' the final book of the trilogy! Also, we're done designing merch for this series, and it should be on sale come January.

Oh, wait, I'm not done yet! I do believe volume 2 of *I Married the Demon Lord's Daughter and Started Living in the Country, but It Seems We're Not Allowed to Be Happy!* will soon go on sale, courtesy of GA Bunko.

I think that's about everything I have to report? Hope I didn't forget anything...

Now then, allow me to offer my gratitude to everyone who has assisted me.

To my chief editor, K, who always takes care of me. To the illustrator, COMTA, who provided the gorgeous illustrations yet again (Kid Nephy is cute, but that dragon was wonderful). To everyone involved with the cover design, proofreading, publicity, and such. To my children, who have been busy with the PTA and cleaning the house. And to you, my dear readers, who are holding this book in your hands.

Thank you very much!

December 2017: On a certain noisy day at the end of the year
— Fuminori Teshima

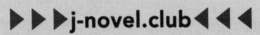

J-Novel Club Lineup

Ebook Releases Series List

Amagi Brilliant Park
An Archdemon's Dilemma:
    How to Love Your Elf Bride
Arifureta Zero
Arifureta: From Commonplace
    to World's Strongest
Ascendance of a Bookworm
Bluesteel Blasphemer
Campfire Cooking in Another World
    with My Absurd Skill
Cooking with Wild Game
Crest of the Stars
Demon King Daimaou
Demon Lord, Retry!
Der Werwolf: The Annals of Veight
From Truant to Anime Screenwriter: My
    Path to "Anohana" and "The Anthem of
    the Heart"
Full Metal Panic!
Grimgar of Fantasy and Ash
How a Realist Hero Rebuilt the Kingdom
How NOT to Summon a Demon Lord
I Saved Too Many Girls and Caused the
    Apocalypse
I Shall Survive Using Potions!
If It's for My Daughter, I'd Even Defeat a
    Demon Lord
In Another World With My Smartphone
Infinite Dendrogram
Infinite Stratos
Invaders of the Rokujouma!?
JK Haru is a Sex Worker in Another World
Kokoro Connect
Last and First Idol
Lazy Dungeon Master
Middle-Aged Businessman, Arise in Another
    World!
Mixed Bathing in Another Dimension
My Big Sister Lives in a Fantasy World
My Next Life as a Villainess: All Routes Lead
    to Doom!
Otherside Picnic
Outbreak Company
Paying to Win in a VRMMO

Record of Wortenia War
Seirei Gensouki: Spirit Chronicles
Seriously Seeking Sister! Ultimate Vampire
    Princess Just Wants Little Sister; Plenty of
    Service Will Be Provided!
Sexiled: My Sexist Party Leader Kicked
    Me Out, So I Teamed Up With a Mythical
    Sorceress!
Side-By-Side Dreamers
Sorcerous Stabber Orphen:
    The Wayward Journey
The Faraway Paladin
The Greatest Magicmaster's Retirement Plan
The Magic in this Other World is
    Too Far Behind!
The Master of Ragnarok & Blesser of Einherjar
The Unwanted Undead Adventurer
There Was No Secret Evil-Fighting
    Organization (srsly?!), So I Made One
    MYSELF!
Welcome to Japan, Ms. Elf!

Manga Series:
A Very Fairy Apartment
An Archdemon's Dilemma:
    How to Love Your Elf Bride
Animeta!
Ascendance of a Bookworm
Cooking with Wild Game
Demon Lord, Retry!
Discommunication
How a Realist Hero Rebuilt the Kingdom
I Shall Survive Using Potions!
Infinite Dendrogram
Marginal Operation
Seirei Gensouki: Spirit Chronicles
Sorcerous Stabber Orphen:
    The Reckless Journey
Sweet Reincarnation
The Faraway Paladin
The Magic in this Other World is
    Too Far Behind!
The Master of Ragnarok & Blesser of Einherjar
The Unwanted Undead Adventurer

An enormous dragon was protecting Zaga and the others. Though, having said that, it wasn't a living, breathing dragon but one made of light woven with mana.

"Ridiculous... It's a... dragon

"Heaven's Scale — Dragon Form!"

Zagan

An orphan who was abducted by a certain sorcerer as a child, but then slaughtered him and stole all his assets and knowledge. After falling in love with Nephy at first sight and purchasing her, he worries over how to properly convey his feelings.

Nephelia

An elf with snow-white hair. Her nickname is Nephy. Even among the elves, who possessed a high level of mana, hers was extraordinarily high, so she was treated as a 'cursed child.' Little by little, she grows to feel affection for Zagan, who told her that 'he needed her'...?

Chastille Lillqvist

A girl who inherited a Sacred Sword, and earned the title Maiden of the Sacred Sword. Though she is a master of the blade, she is far too serious and thus easily deceived. After failing to subjugate a sorcerer, she was saved by Zagan, and is now conflicted by her feelings for him, a sorcerer who is made out to be evil.

Valefor

A young dragon who attacked Zagan to steal his Archdemon powers because she desires strength. Her nickname is Foll. After Zagan turns the tables on her, she is forced to stay at the castle and help Nephy with chores.

Nephy had turned into a small child.

AN ARCHDEMON'S DILEMMA: HOW TO LOVE YOUR ELF BRIDE